POP GEMS OF THE 1950s

CONTENTS

— PIANO LEVEL —
EARLY INTERMEDIATE/INTERMEDIATE
(HLSPL LEVEL 4-5)

ISBN 978-1-4234-2563-2

7777 W. Bluemound Rd. P.O.Box 13819 Milwaukee, WI 53213

Visit Hal Leonard Online at
www.halleonard.com

Visit Phillip at
www.phillipkeveren.com

PREFACE

From crooners like Nat King Cole and Frank Sinatra to rock 'n' rollers like Bill Haley and Elvis Presley, the 1950s brought us a wide variety of popular music. This decade of hula hoops and poodle skirts has long enjoyed a reminiscent place in our popular culture, from movies (*Grease*) to television (*Happy Days*) to an ongoing fascination with all things Elvis. Songs made popular in the '50s continue to reappear on the *Billboard* charts, confirming the notion that this decade served up a treasure trove of timeless tunes.

This collection brings together some of the best songs from this bygone era. I hope you enjoy them!

Sincerely,
Phillip Keveren

BIOGRAPHY

Phillip Keveren, a multi-talented keyboard artist and composer, has composed original works in a variety of genres from piano solo to symphonic orchestra. Mr. Keveren gives frequent concerts and workshops for teachers and their students in the United States, Canada, Europe, and Asia. Mr. Keveren holds a B.M. in composition from California State University Northridge and a M.M. in composition from the University of Southern California.

ALL I HAVE TO DO IS DREAM

Words and Music by
BOUDLEAUX BRYANT
Arranged by Phillip Keveren

Tenderly (𝅗𝅥 = 46)

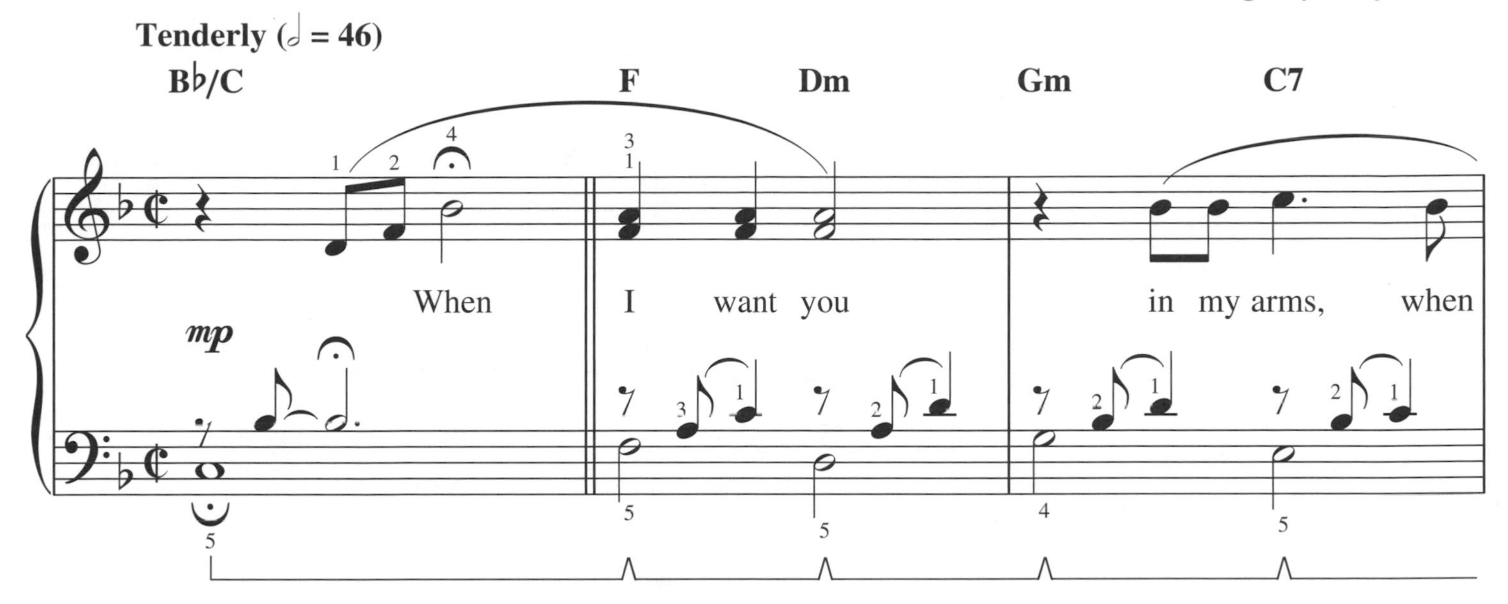

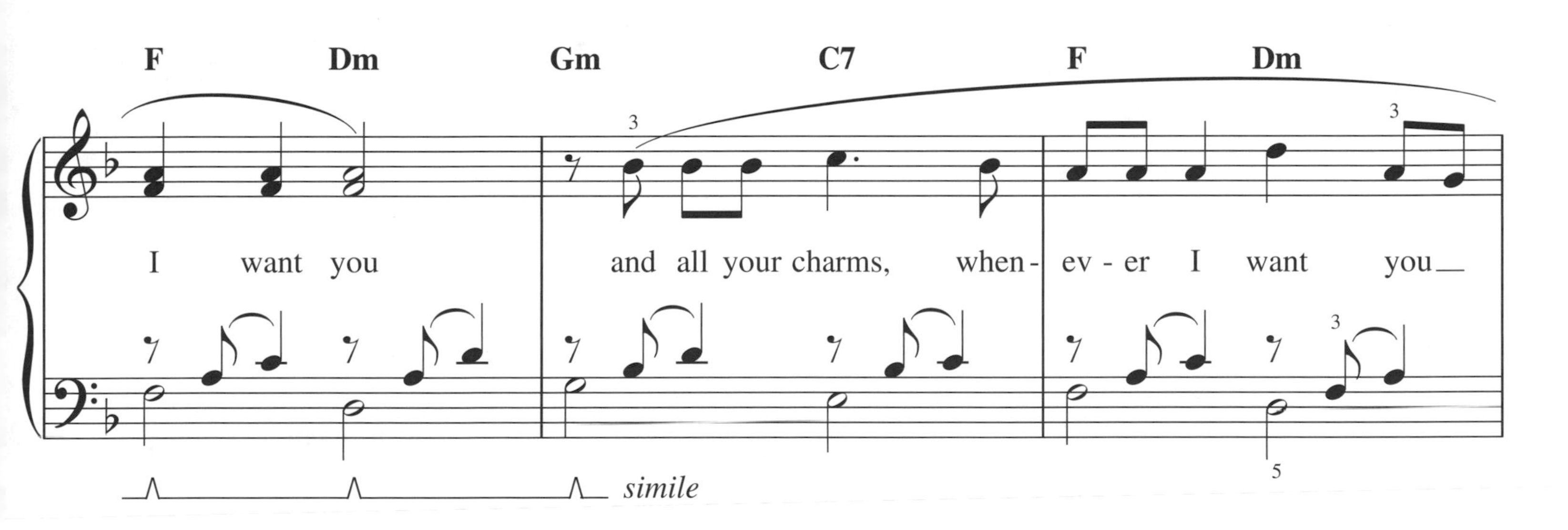

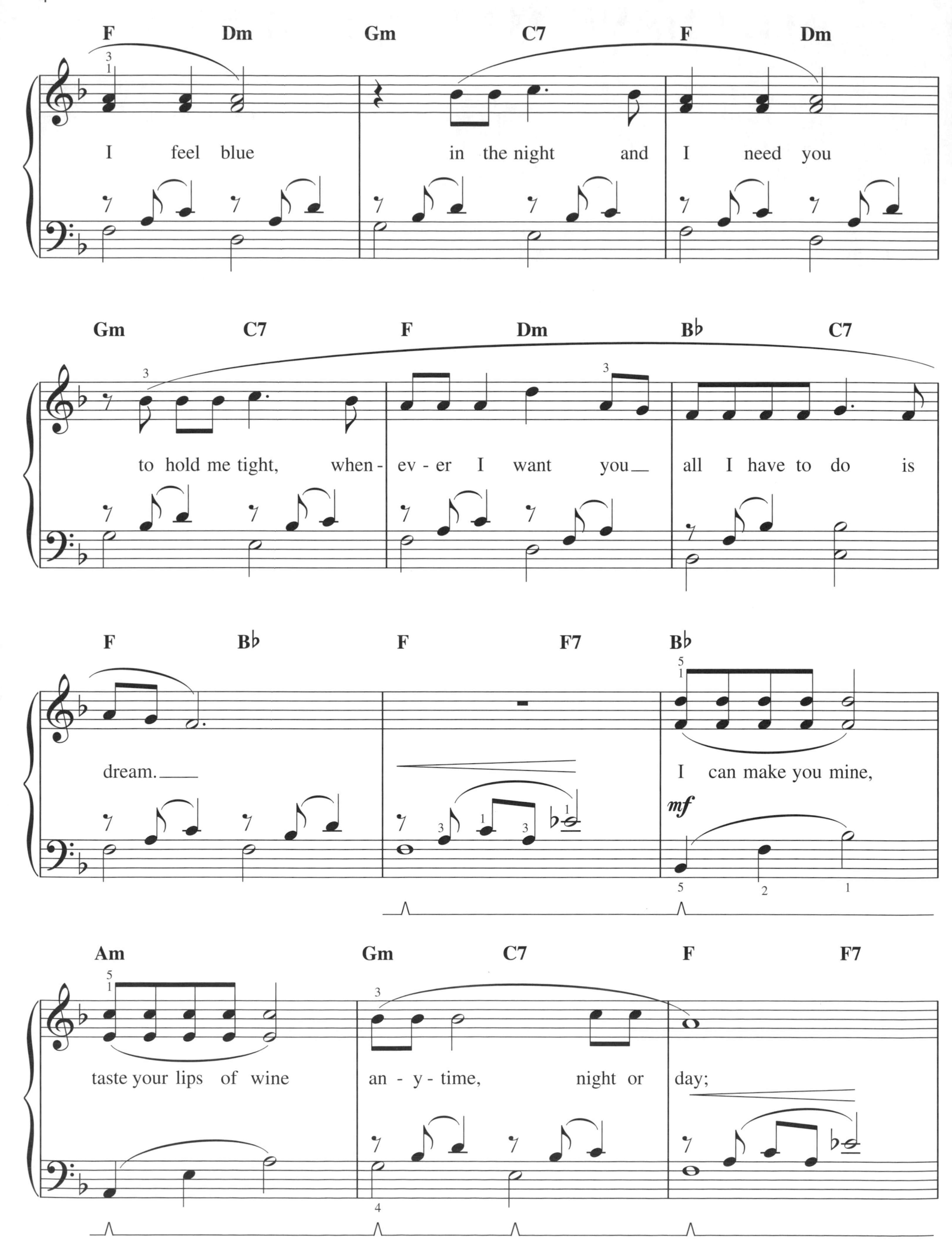
F Dm Gm C7 F Dm
I feel blue in the night and I need you
Gm C7 F Dm B♭ C7
to hold me tight, when - ev - er I want you all I have to do is
F B♭ F F7 B♭
dream.
I can make you mine,
mf
Am Gm C7 F F7
taste your lips of wine an - y - time, night or day;

B♭ Am G7
on - ly trou - ble is, gee whiz, I'm dream - ing my whole life a -
f
C7 F Dm Gm C7 F Dm
way. I need you so that I could die. I love you so
rit.
mp
a tempo
Gm C7 F Dm B♭ C7
and that is why when - ev - er I want you all I have to do is
F Dm Gm C7 F B♭ F
dream. All I have to do is dream.
rit.

FEVER

Words and Music by JOHN DAVENPORT
and EDDIE COOLEY
Arranged by Phillip Keveren

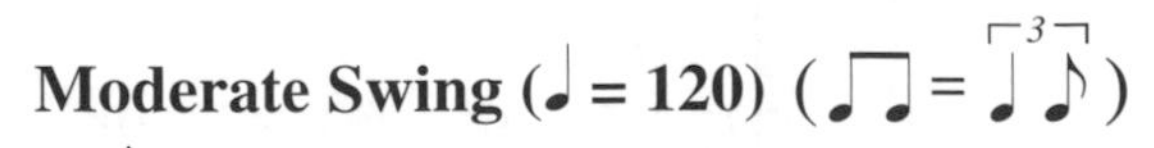

when you kiss me, fe - ver when you hold me

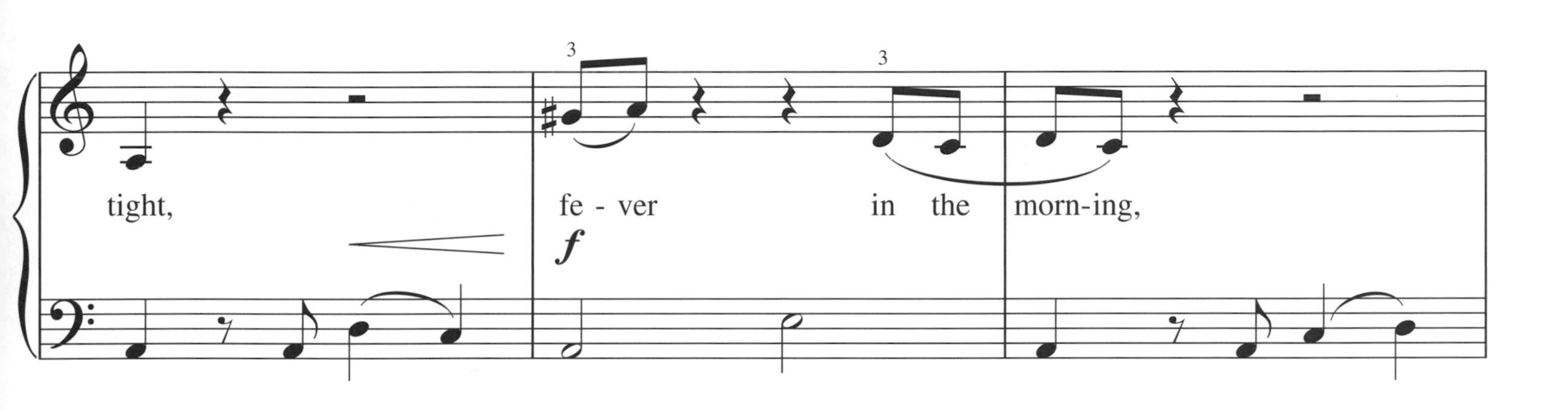
tight, fe - ver in the morn-ing,
f

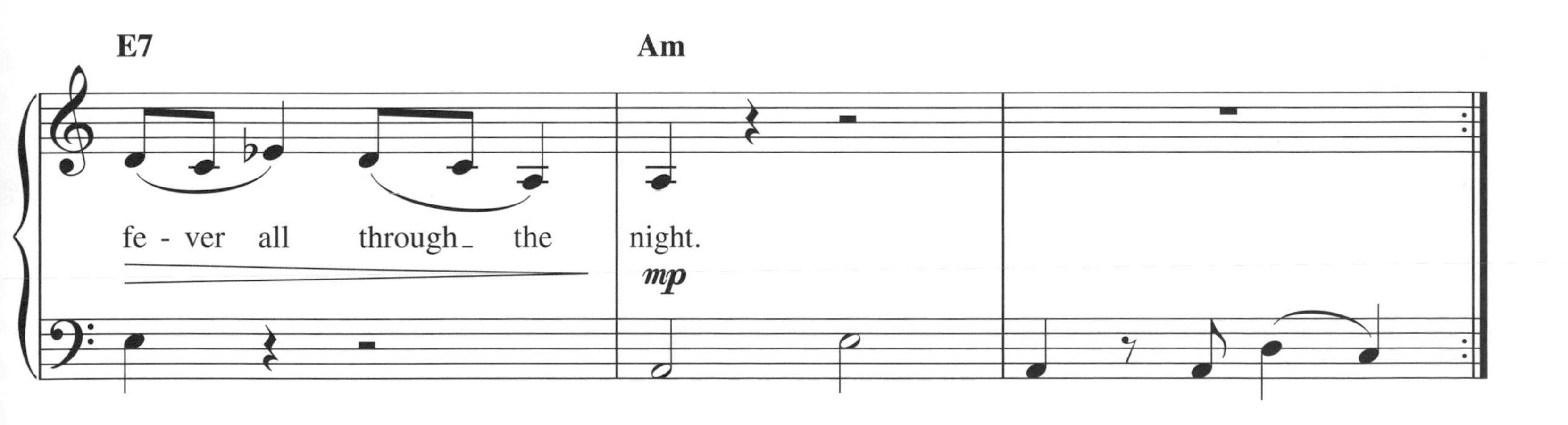
E7
Am
fe - ver all through the night.
mp

R.H. snap fingers

IT'S ALL IN THE GAME

Lyrics by CARL SIGMAN
Music by CHARLES GATES DAWES
Arranged by Phillip Keveren

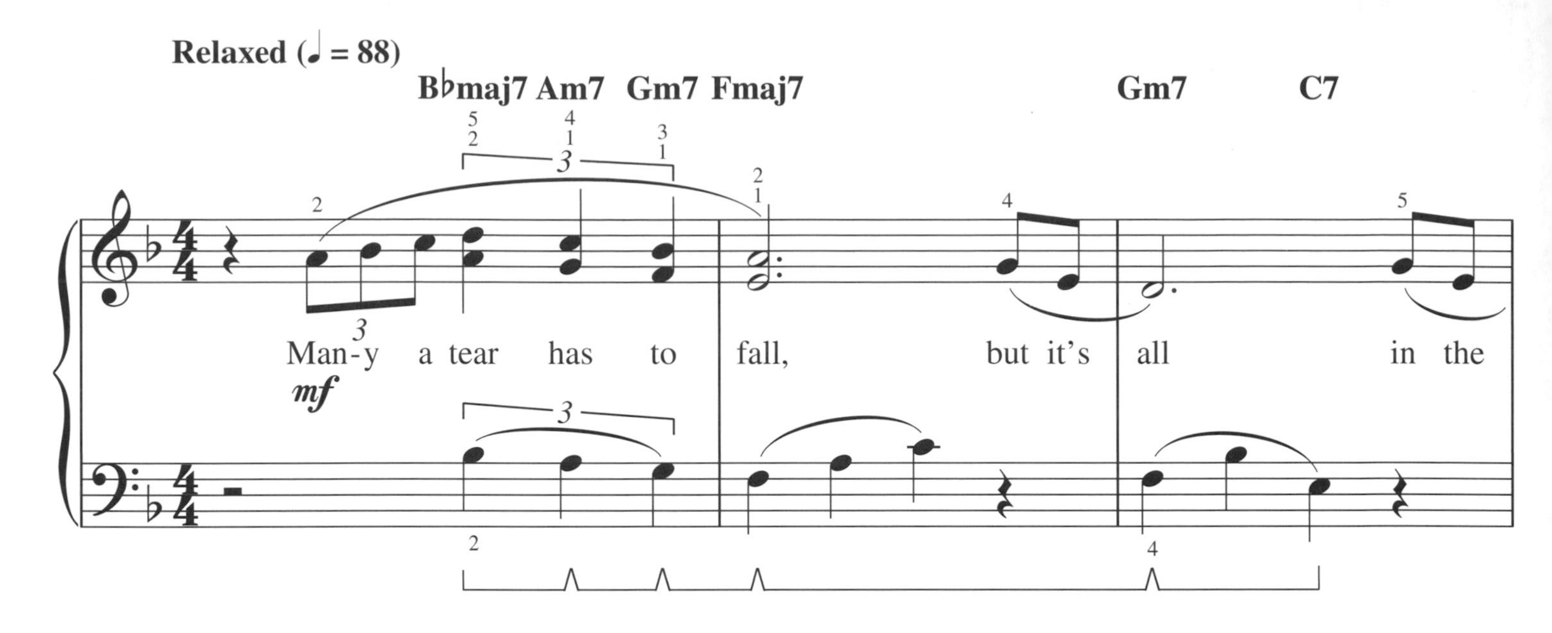

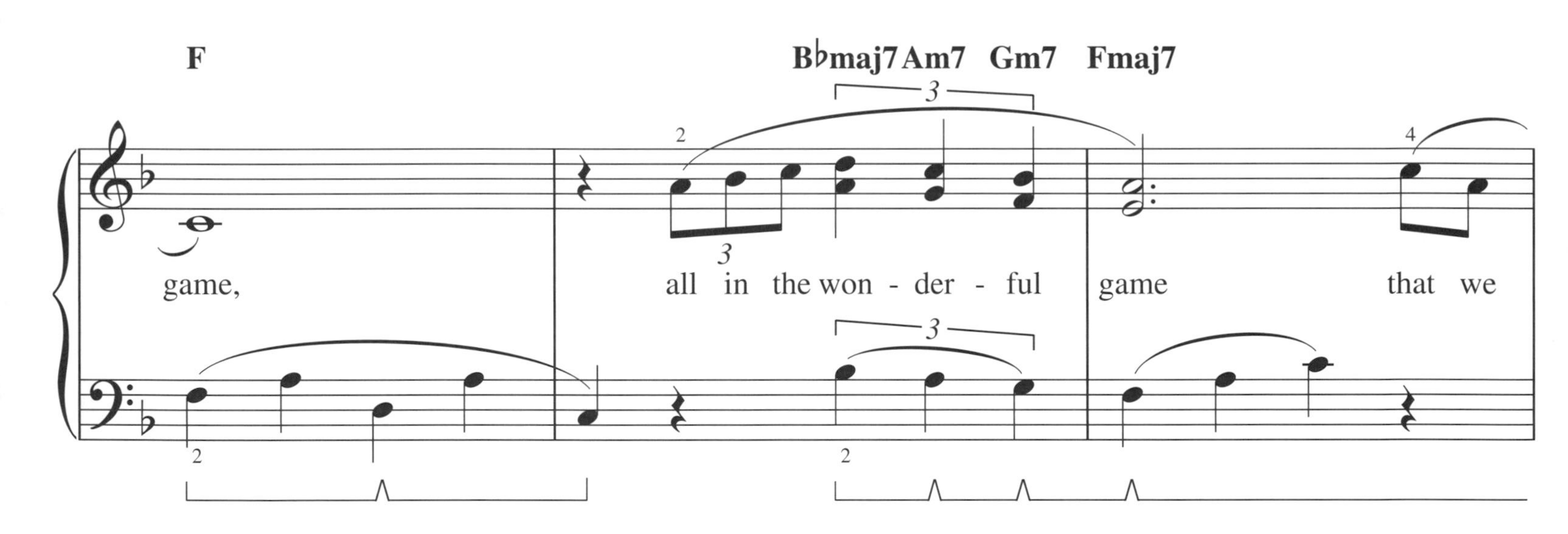

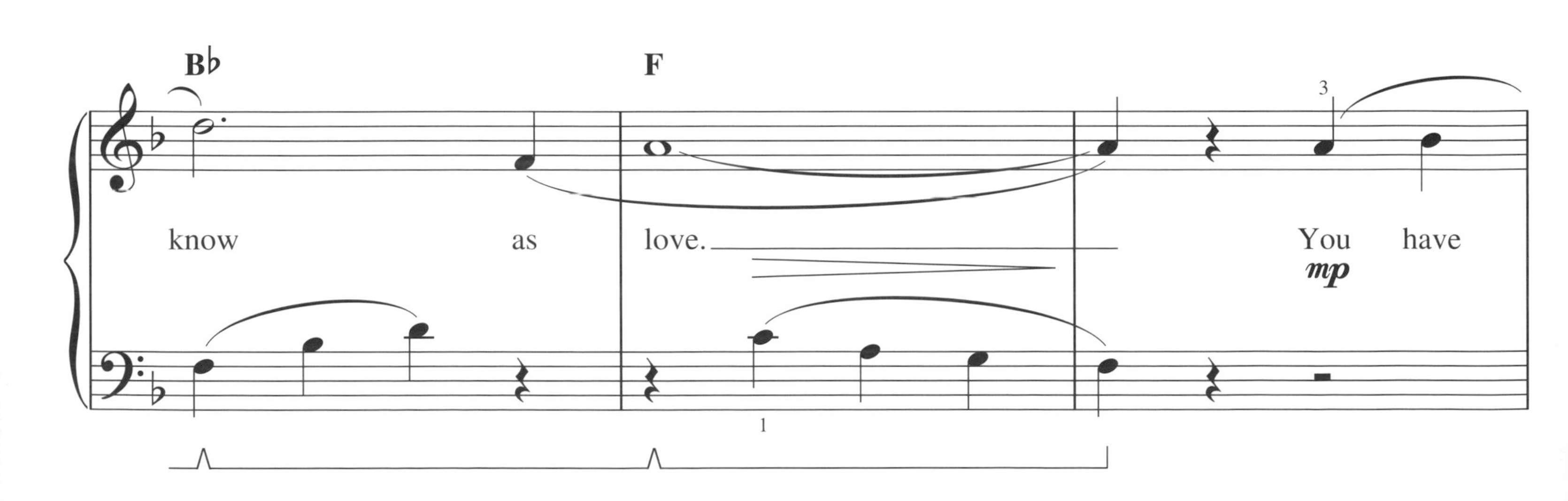

G7
words with him and your fu - ture's look - ing
C Fm C F♯dim C Dm G7
dim, but these things your hearts can rise a -
C Cdim C7 B♭maj7 Am7 Gm7 Fmaj7
bove. Once in a while he won't call, but it's
Gm7 C7 F B♭maj7 Am7 Gm7
all in the game. Soon he'll be there at your

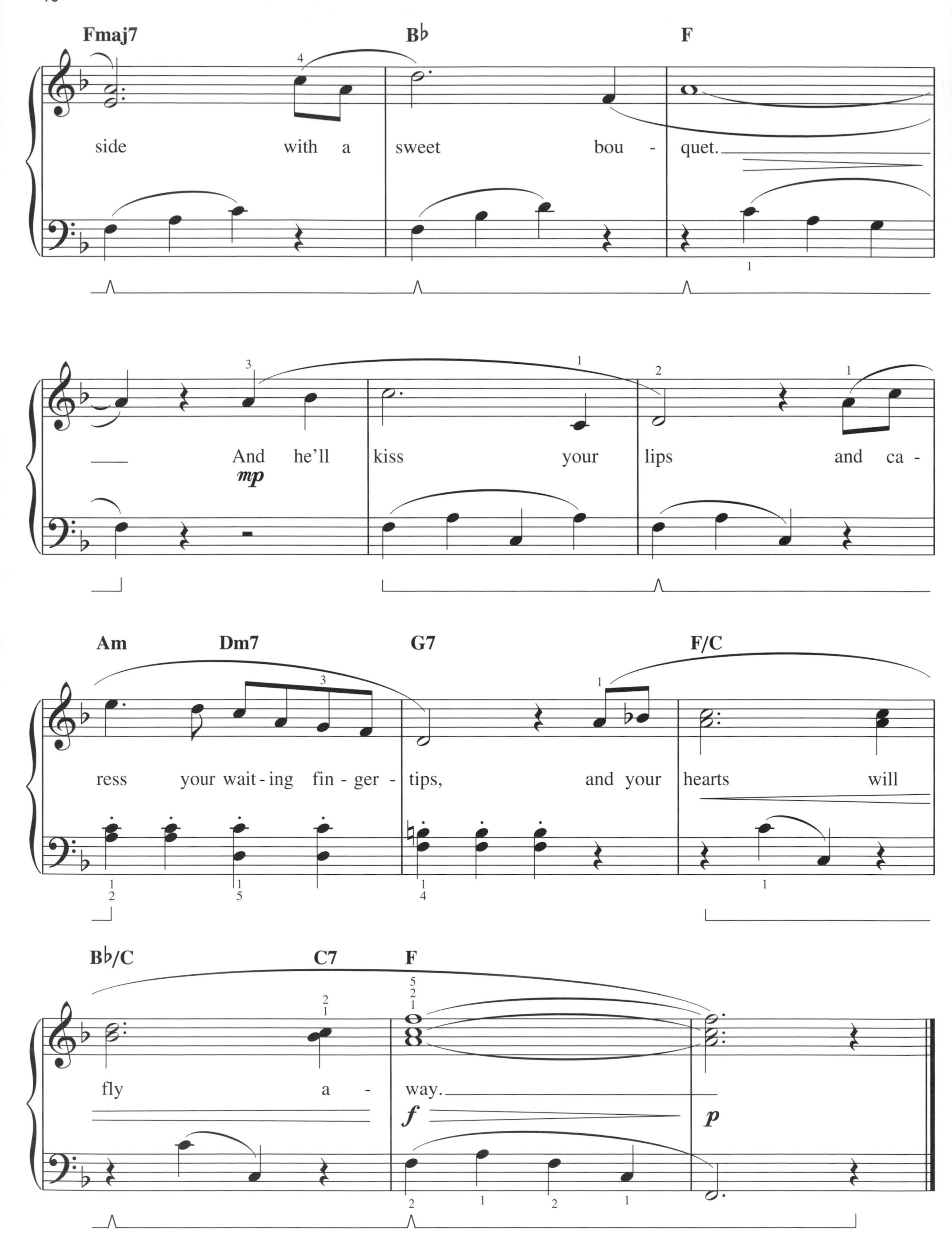
Fmaj7
B♭
F
side with a sweet bou - quet.
And he'll kiss your lips and ca -
mp
Am
Dm7
G7
F/C
ress your wait - ing fin - ger - tips, and your hearts will
B♭/C
C7
F
fly a - way.
f
p

IT'S NOT FOR ME TO SAY

Words by AL STILLMAN
Music by ROBERT ALLEN
Arranged by Phillip Keveren

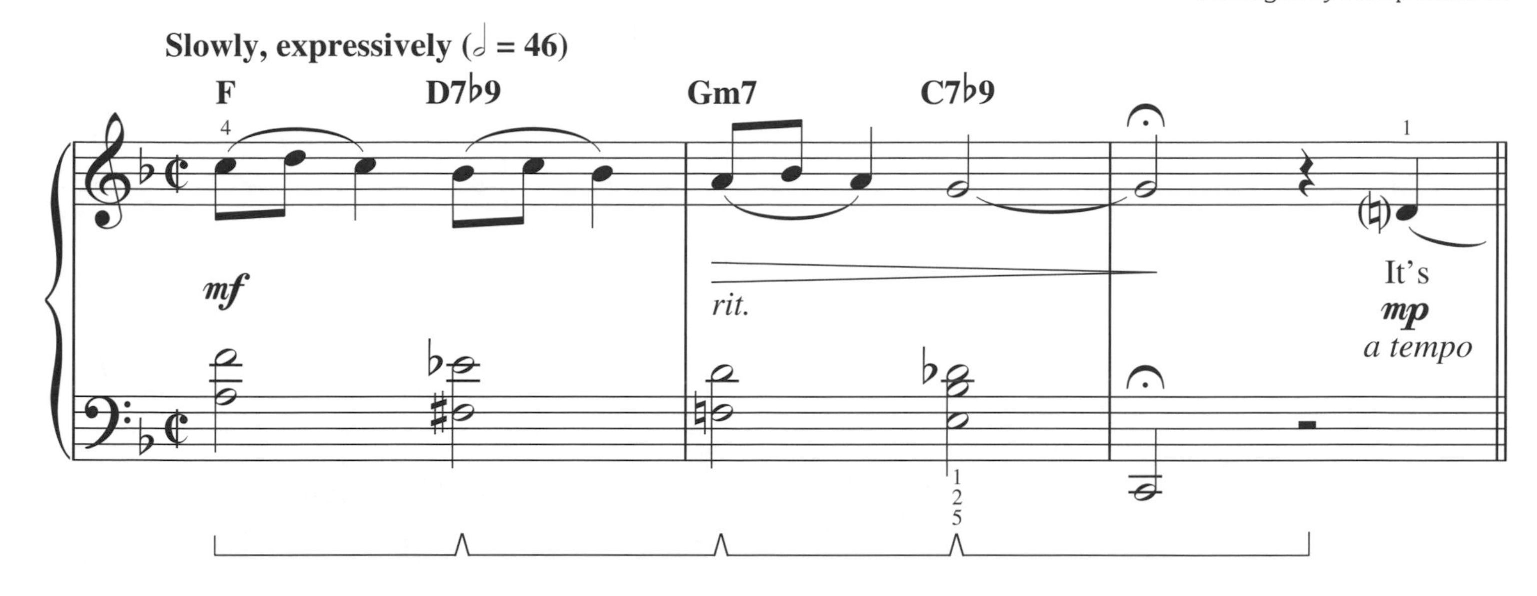

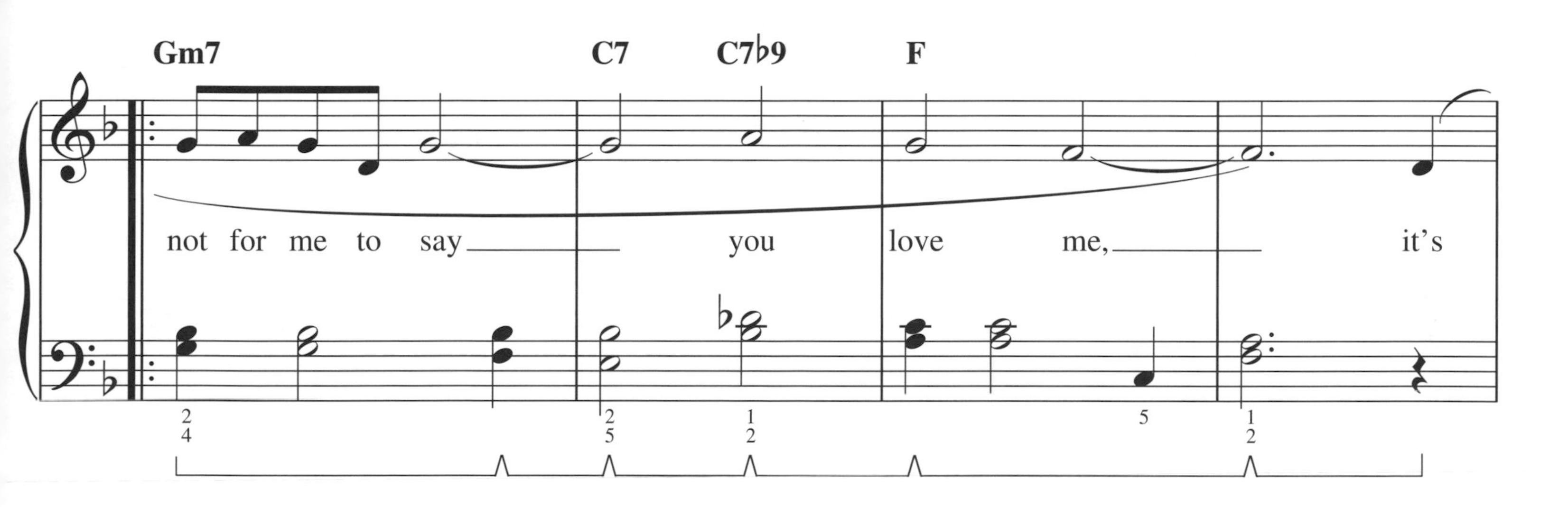

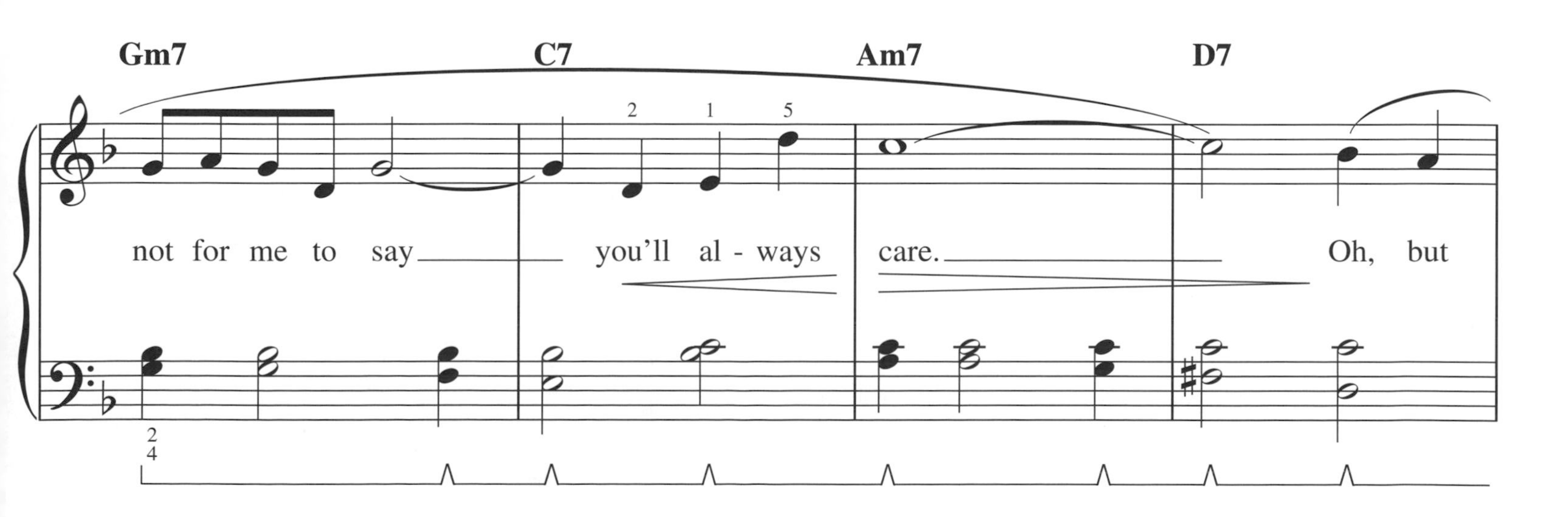

Gm Gm7 Em7♭5 A7 Dm Dm(maj7) Dm7 G7
here for the mo - ment I can hold you fast, and press your
simile
A F♯7 Bm E7 A Gm7 C7
lips to mine, and dream that love will last. As
Gm7 C7 C7♭9 F
far as I can see, this is heav - en, and
Cm7 F F+ B♭maj7 B♭6
speak-ing just for me, it's ours to share; per -

B♭maj7
B♭m
Am7
haps the glow of love will grow with ev - 'ry pass - ing day,
f
1.
D7
G7
C7
or we may nev - er meet a - gain, but then, it's not for me to
dim.
F
say.
It's
mp
2.
D7
D7♭9
or we may
mp
Gm7
C7
F
F6
nev - er meet a - gain, but then, it's not for me to say.
rit.
pp

LOVE ME TENDER

Words and Music by ELVIS PRESLEY
and VERA MATSON
Arranged by Phillip Keveren

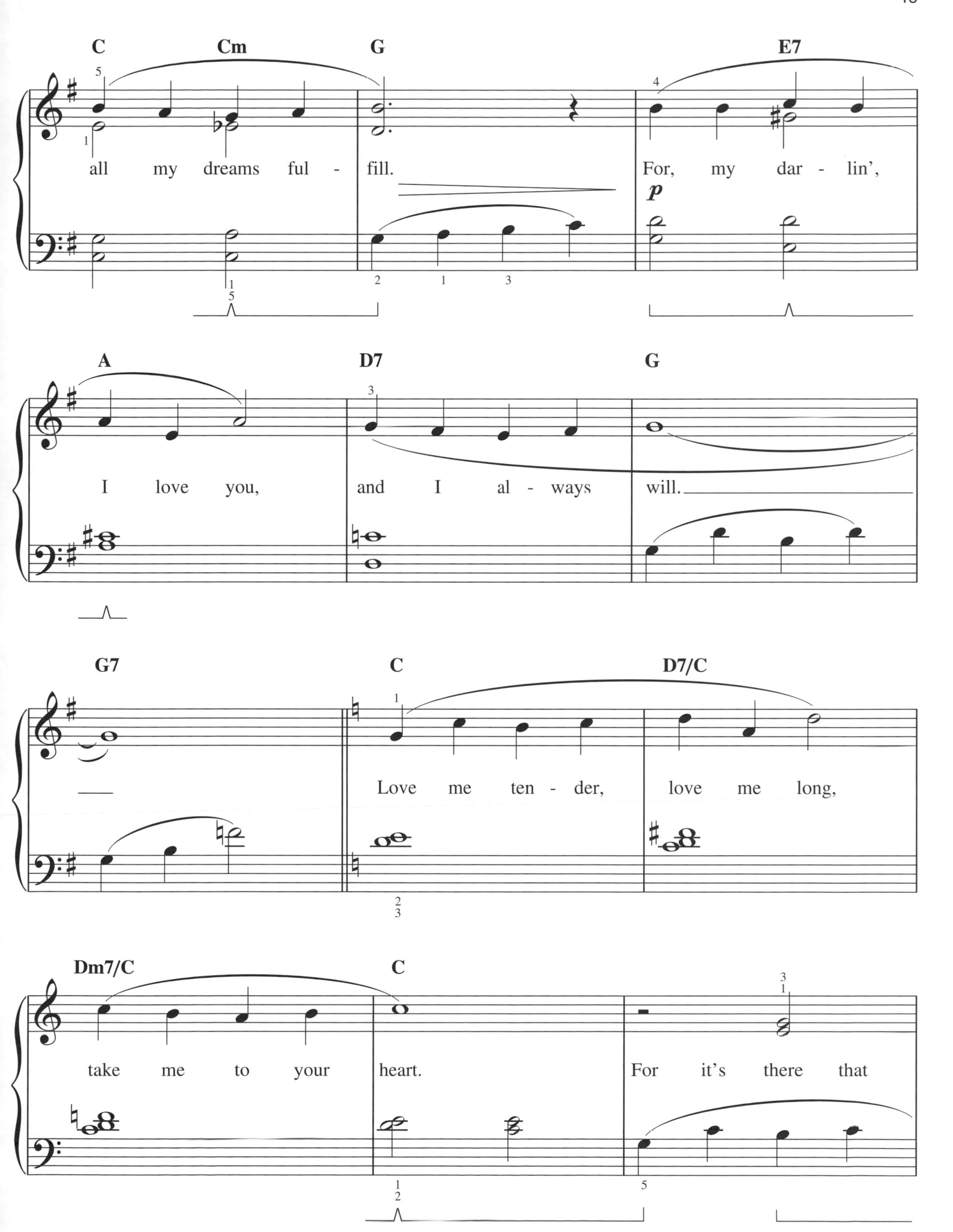
C Cm G E7
all my dreams ful - fill.
For, my dar - lin',
p
A D7 G
I love you, and I al - ways will.
G7 C D7/C
Love me ten - der, love me long,
Dm7/C C
take me to your heart.
For it's there that

D7 G7 C
I be - long, and we'll nev - er part.
C C+ C6 C7 F Fm
Love me ten - der, love me true, all my dreams ful -
mf
C A7 D
fill. For, my dar - lin', I love you,
p
G7 G7♭9 C
and I al - ways will.
rit.
pp

MOMENTS TO REMEMBER

Words by AL STILLMAN
Music by ROBERT ALLEN
Arranged by Phillip Keveren

Slowly, expressively (♩ = 92)

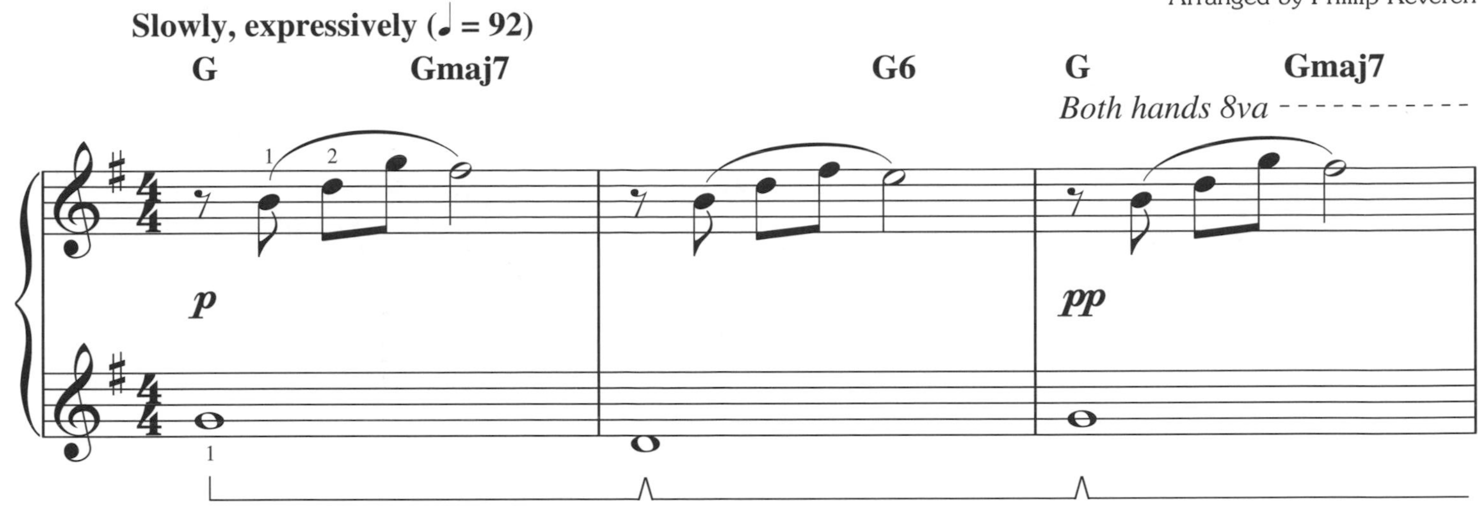

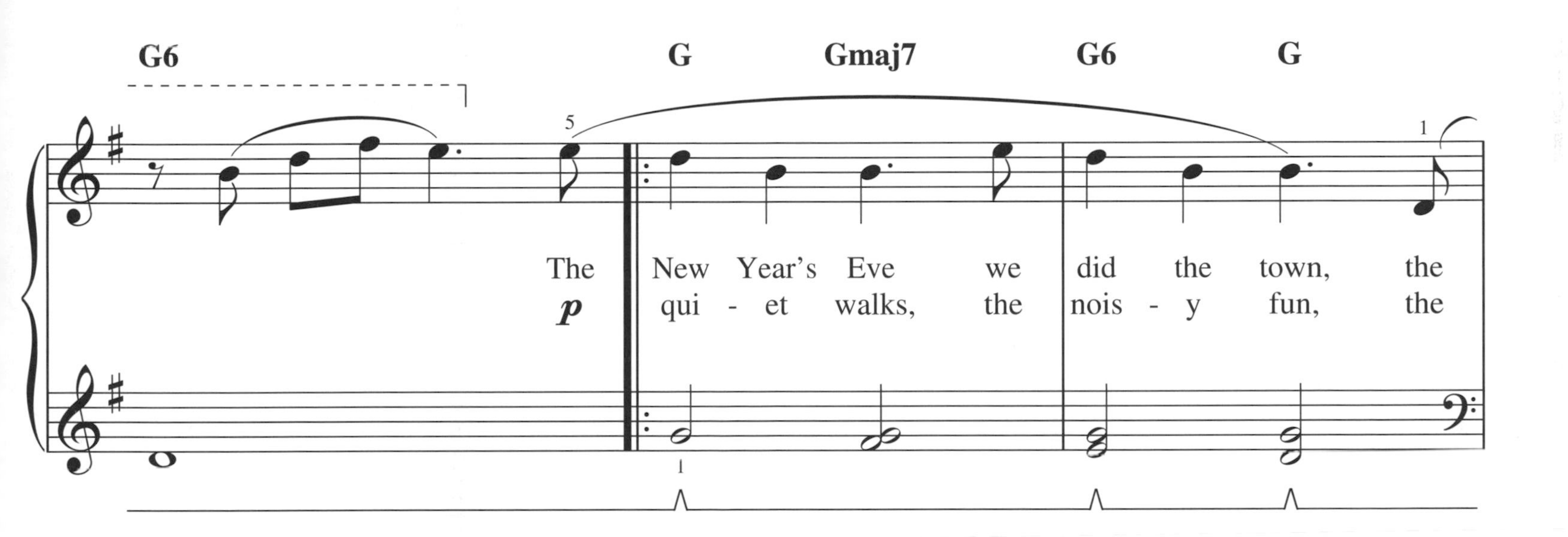

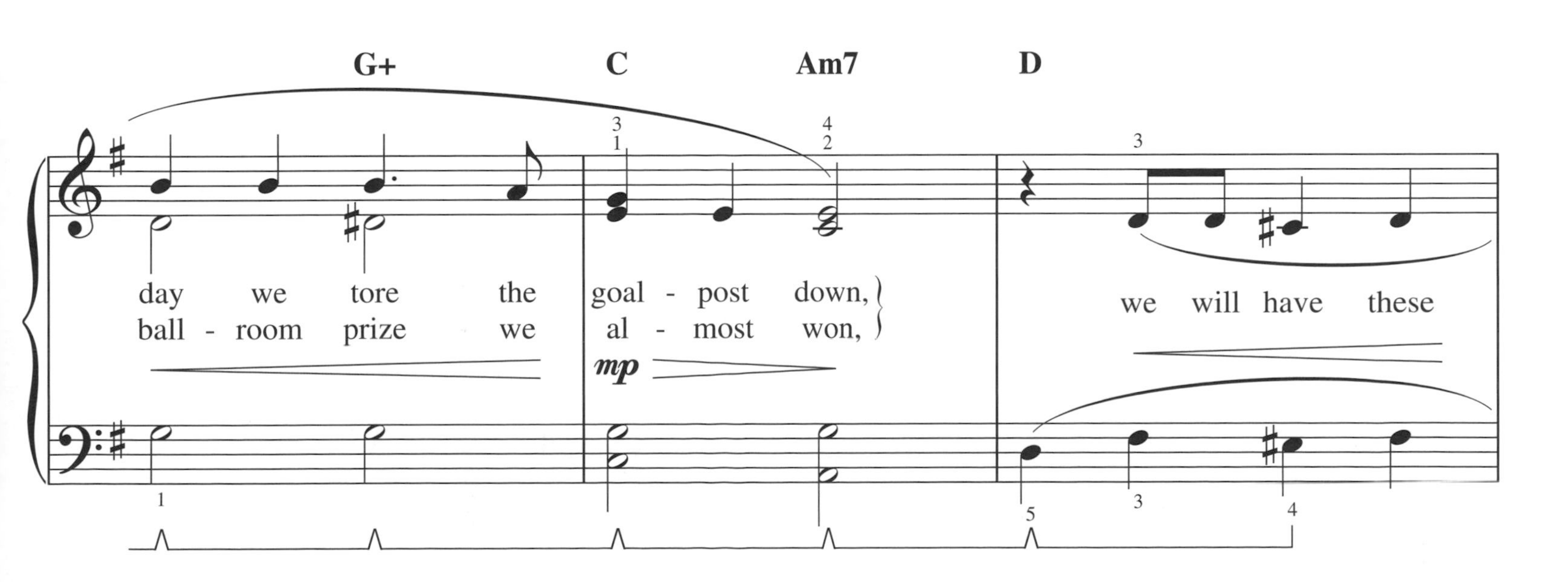

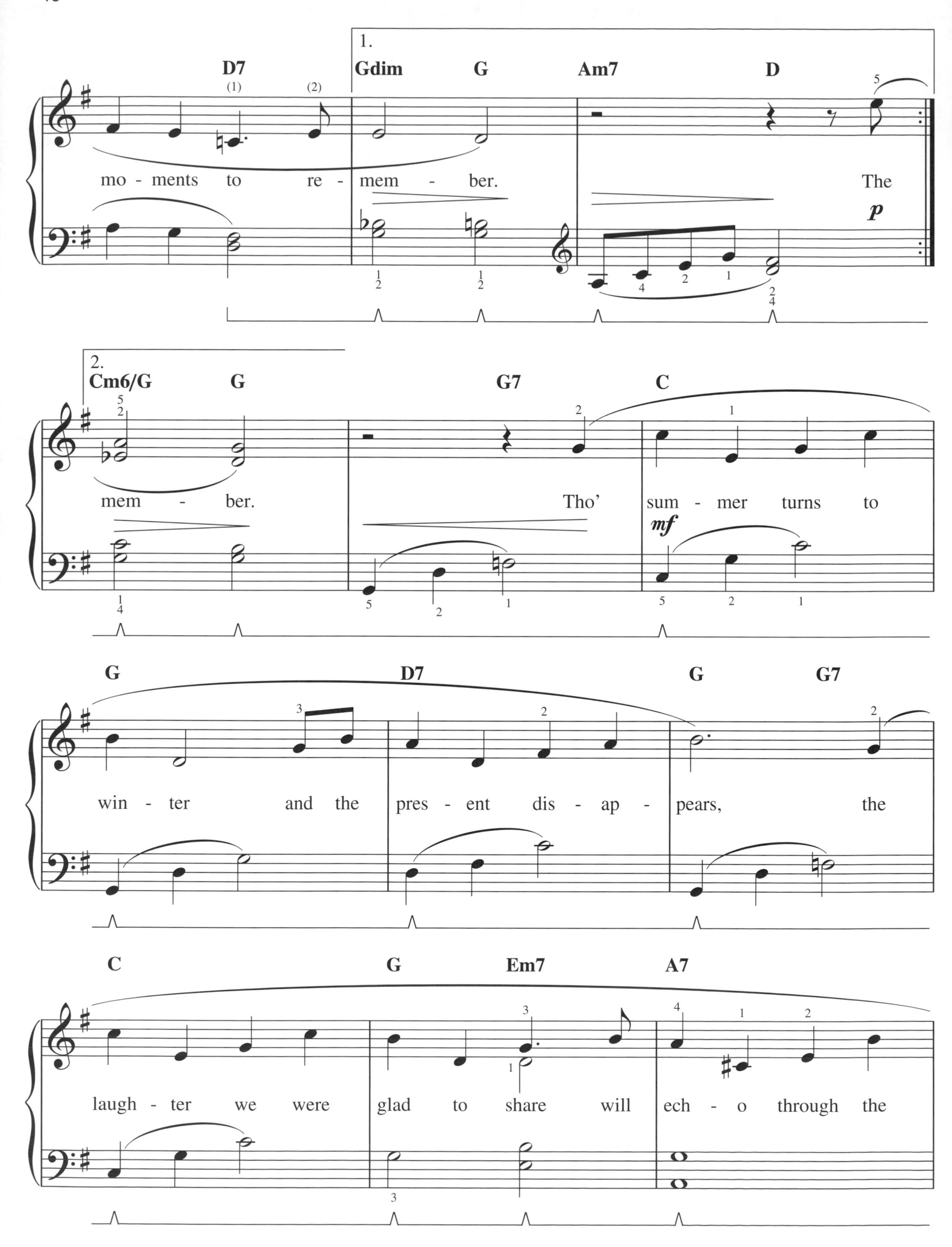
D7 1. Gdim G Am7 D
mo - ments to re - mem - ber. The
p
2. Cm6/G G G7 C
mem - ber. Tho' sum - mer turns to
mf
G D7 G G7
win - ter and the pres - ent dis - ap - pears, the
C G Em7 A7
laugh - ter we were glad to share will ech - o through the

Dsus D G Gmaj7 G6 G
years. When oth - er nights and oth - er days may
poco rit. p a tempo
G G7♯5 C6/9 Am7 D
find us gone our sep - 'rate ways, we will have these
mf cresc.
D7 Cm6/G G Gmaj7
mo - ments to re - mem - ber.
f p
G6 G Gmaj7 G6 G6/9
Both hands 8va
pp rit. mp

PUT YOUR HEAD ON MY SHOULDER

Words and Music by
PAUL ANKA
Arranged by Phillip Keveren

Gm7
C7
F
Dm
Gm7
C7
Won't you miss me once,
ba - by?
Just a kiss good-night,
F
Dm
Gm7
C7
F
B♭
may - be
you and I will fall in
love.
F
C7
F/C
Peo - ple say that
love's a game, a
p
C7
F/C
E7
game you just can't
win.
If
there's a way, I'll
cresc.

Am/E
Gm7
C7
find it some-day, and then this fool will rush in.
f
Dm
Gm7
C7
Put your head on my shoul - der, whis-per in my ear,
mf
F
Dm
Gm7
C7
F
Dm
ba - by, words I want to hear. Tell me,
Gm7
C7
F
B♭
F
G/F
tell me that you love me, too.
rit.
pp

QUE SERA, SERA

(Whatever Will Be, Will Be)

Words and Music by JAY LIVINGSTON
and RAY EVANS
Arranged by Phillip Keveren

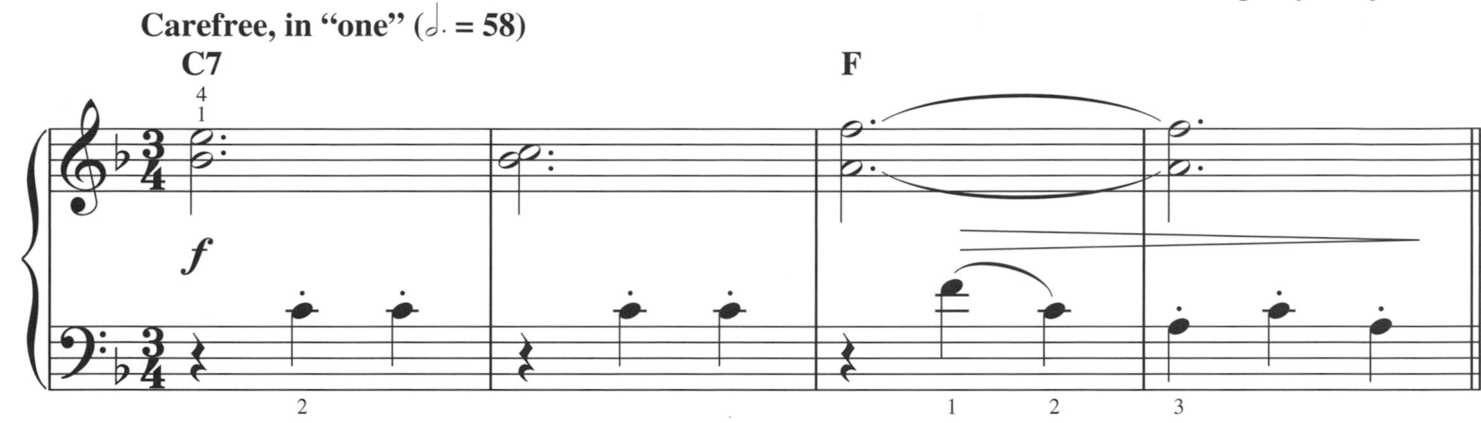

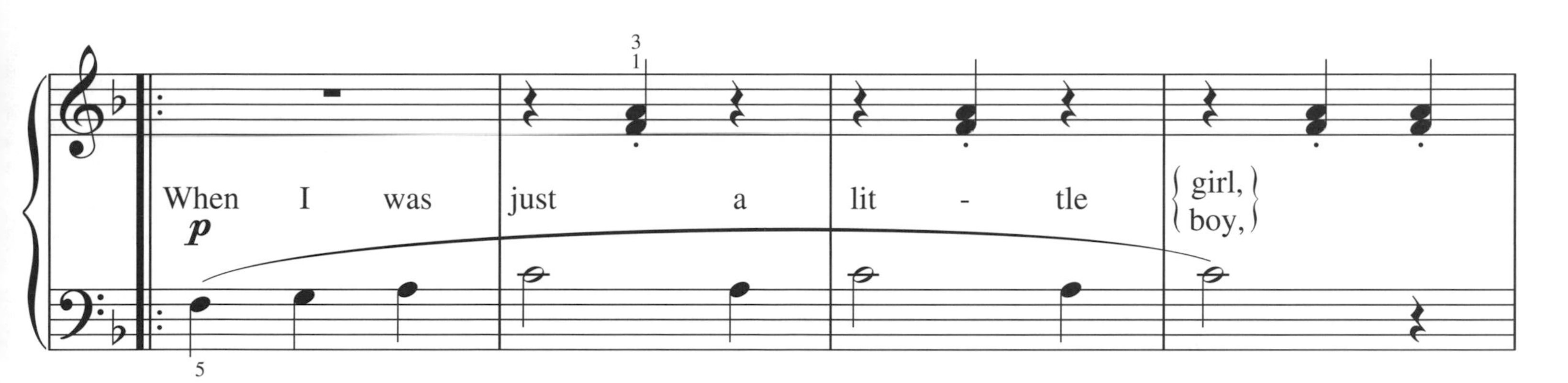

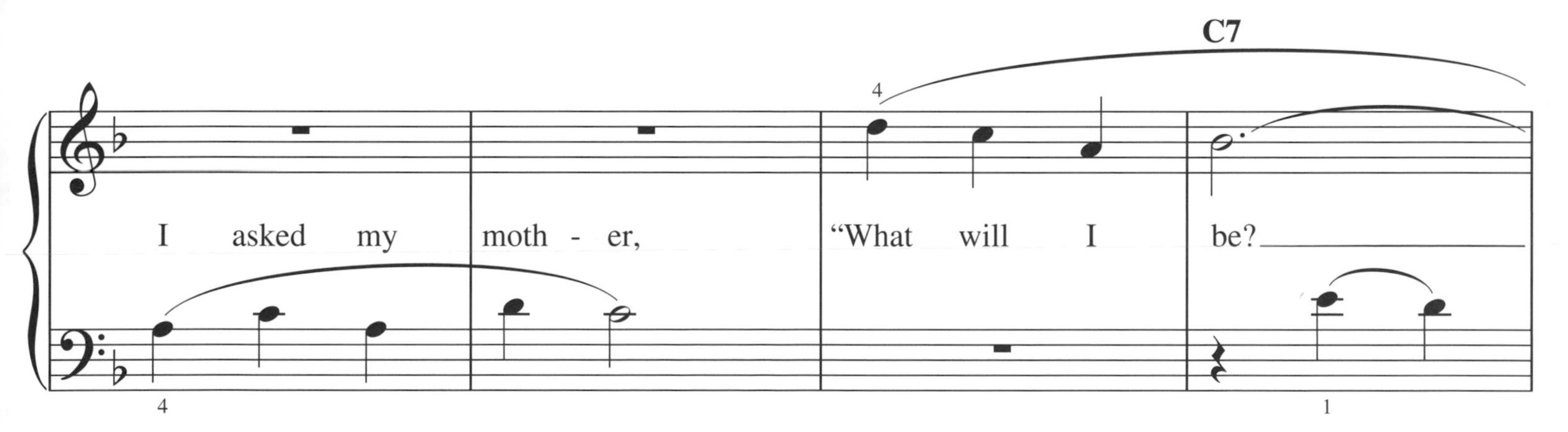

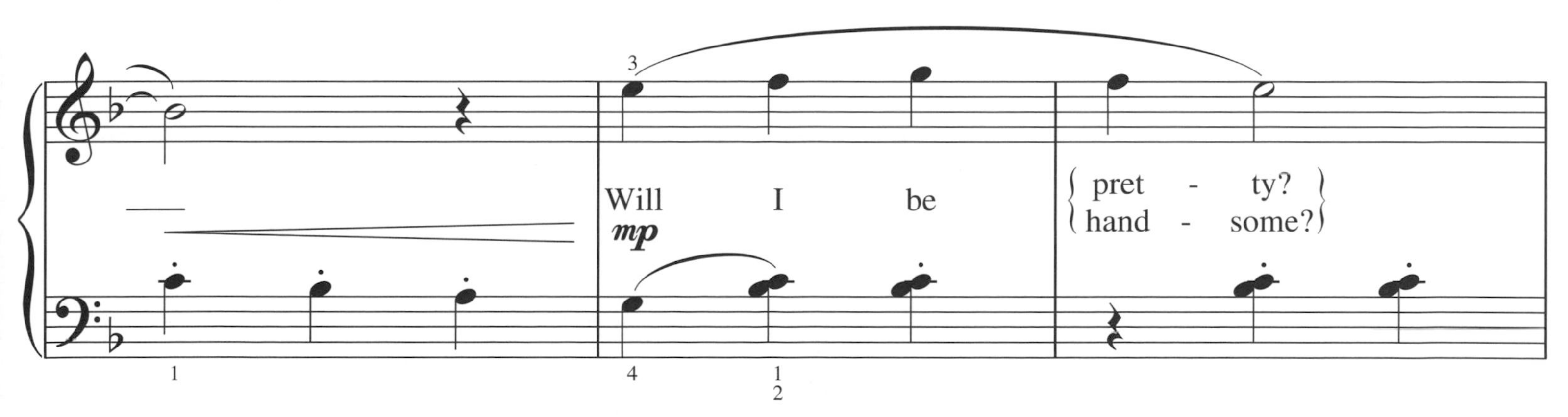

Will I be rich?"
Here's what she said to

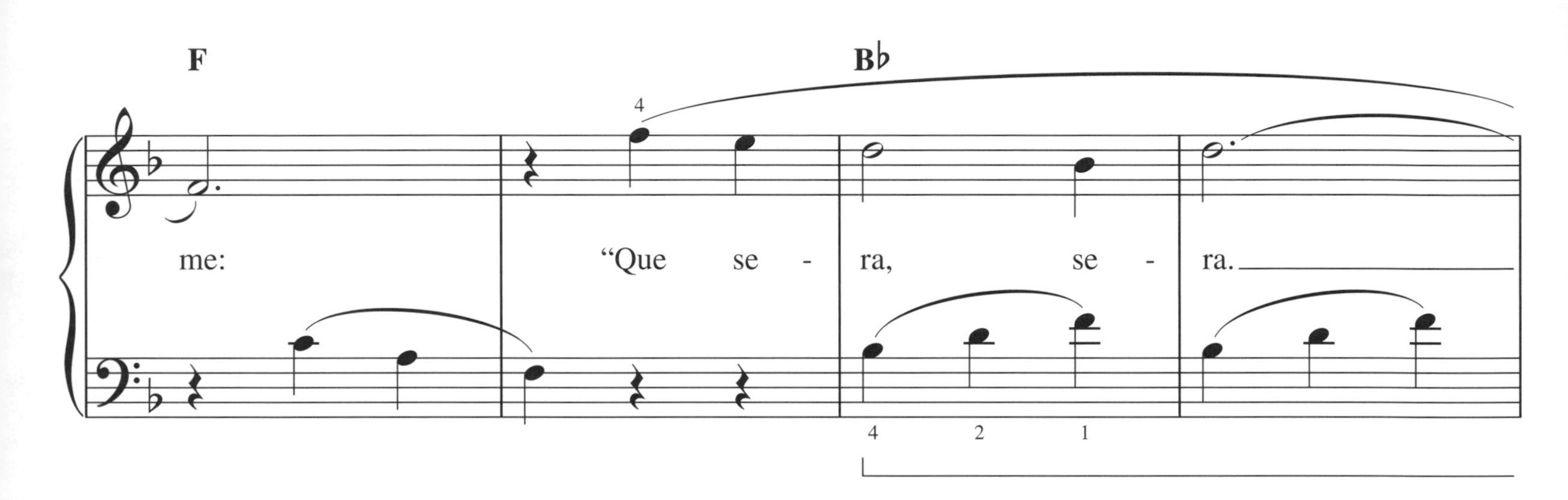
F
B♭
me:
"Que se - ra, se - ra.

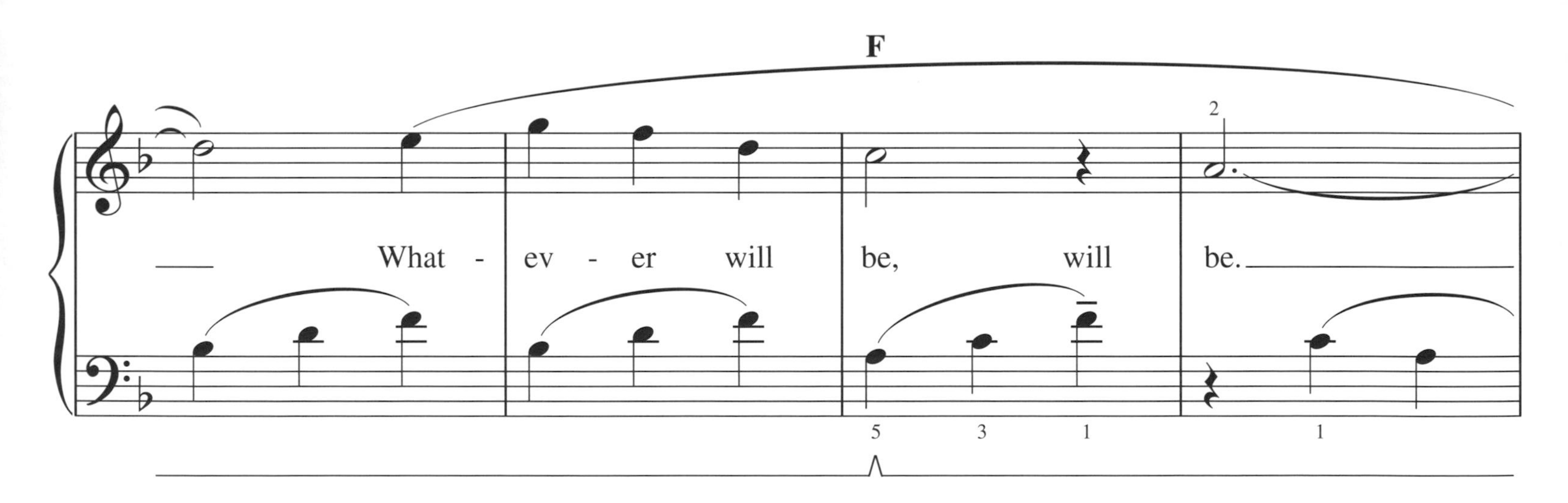
F
What - ev - er will be, will be.

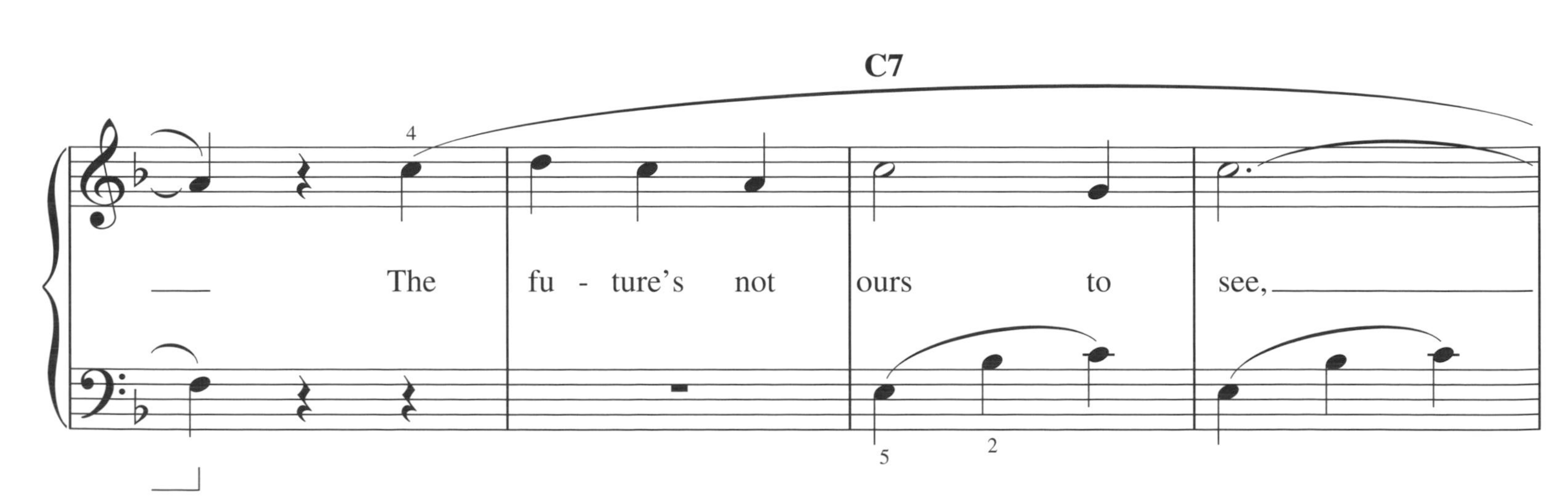
C7
The fu - ture's not ours to see,

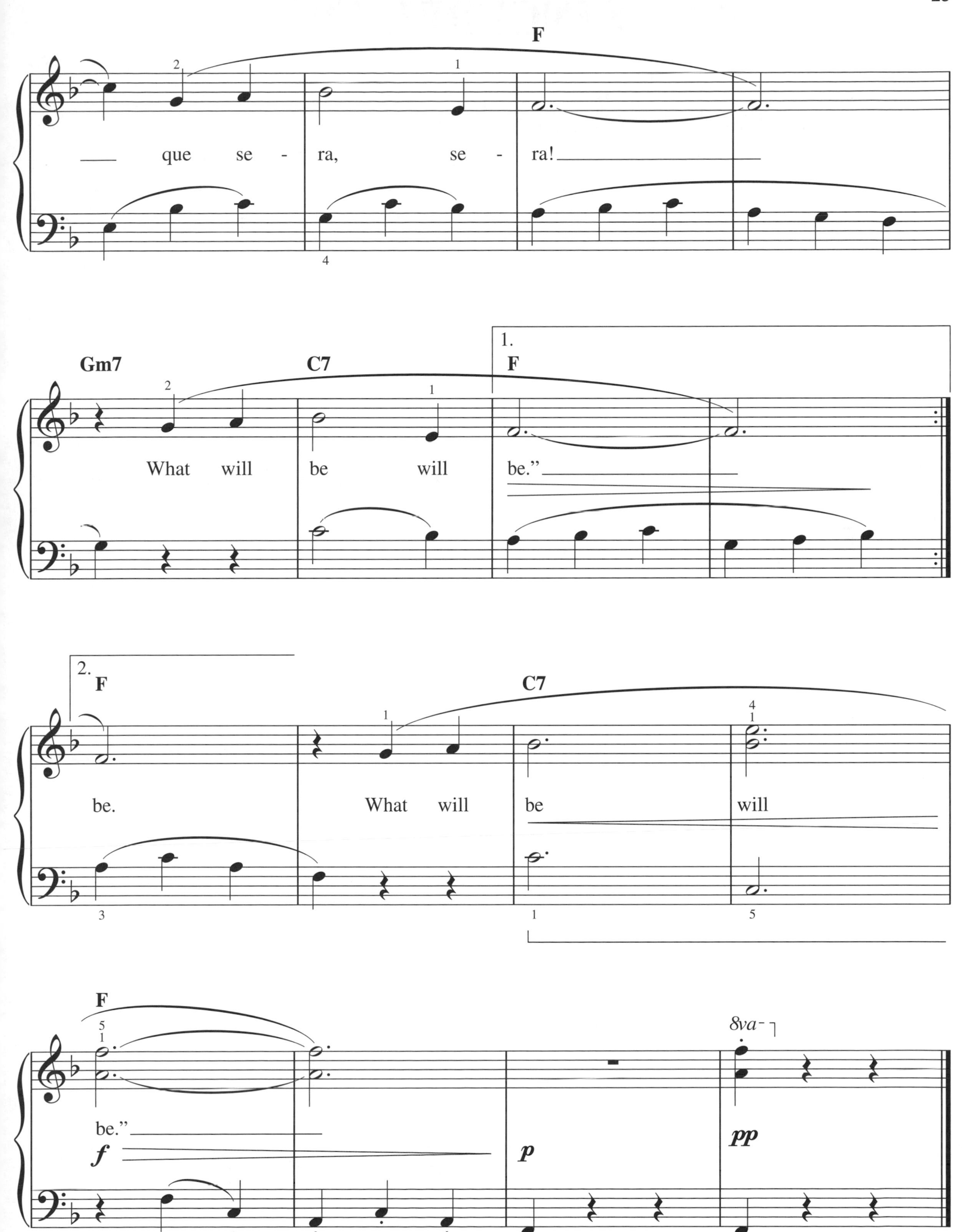
F
que se - ra, se - ra!
Gm7
C7
1.
F
What will be will be."
2.
F
C7
be. What will be will
F
be."
8va
p
f
pp

SINCERELY

Words and Music by ALAN FREED
and HARVEY FUQUA
Arranged by Phillip Keveren

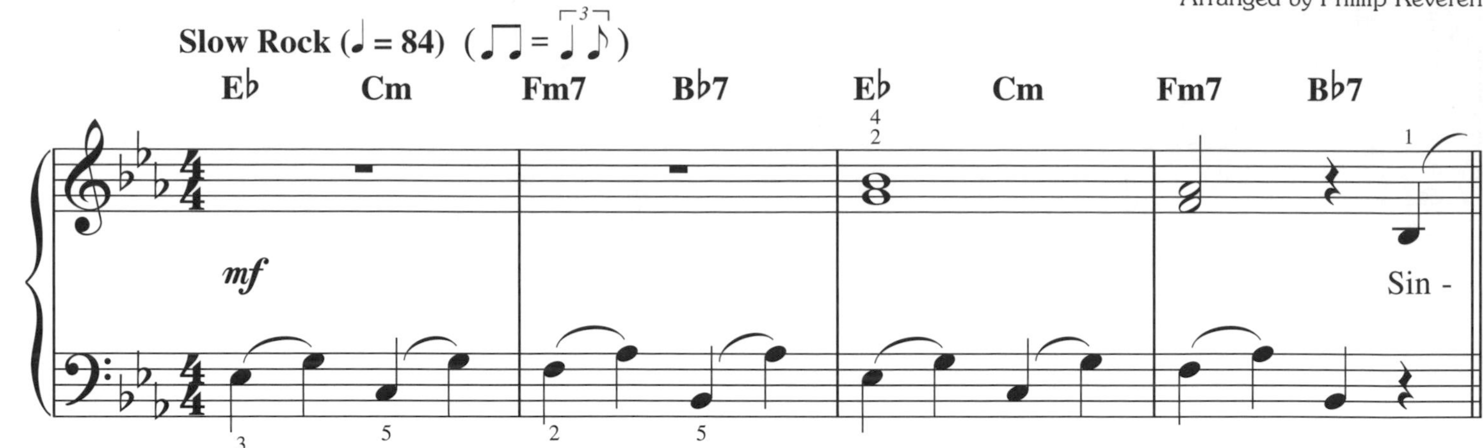

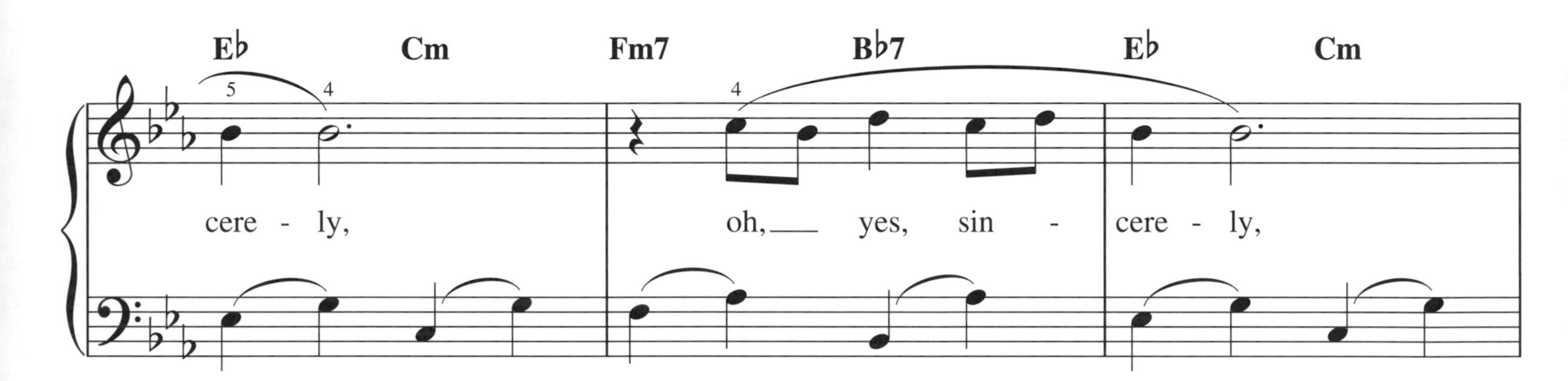

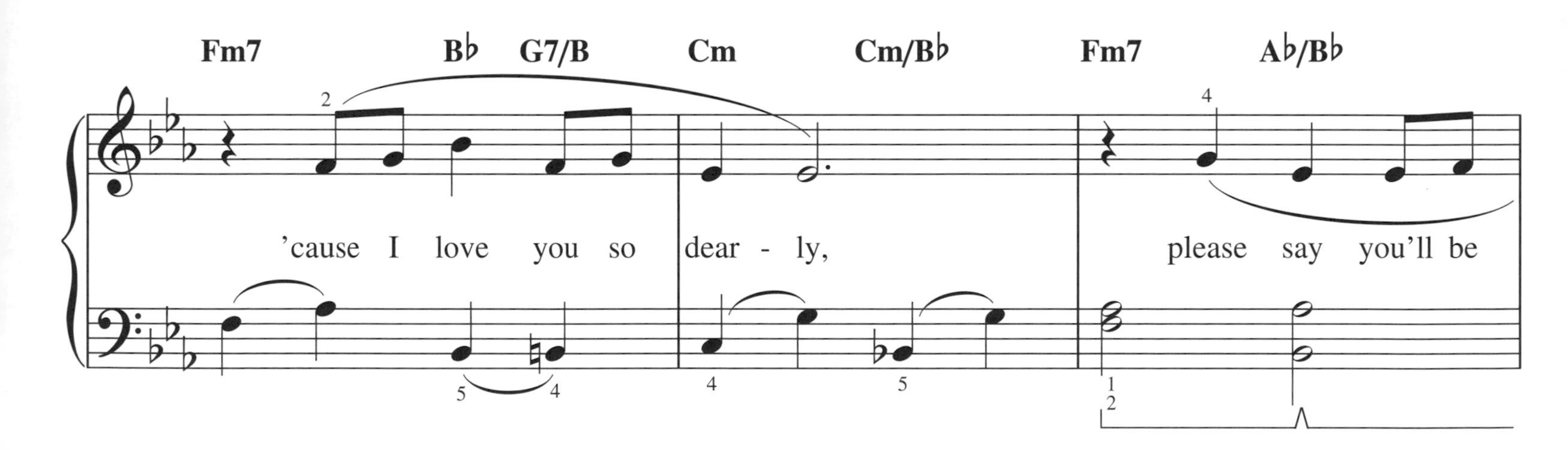

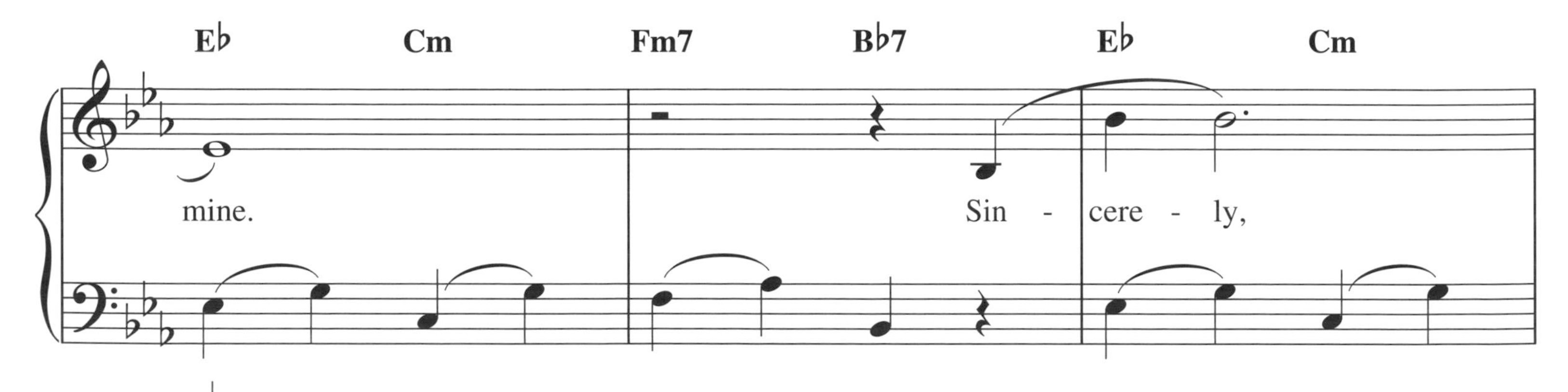

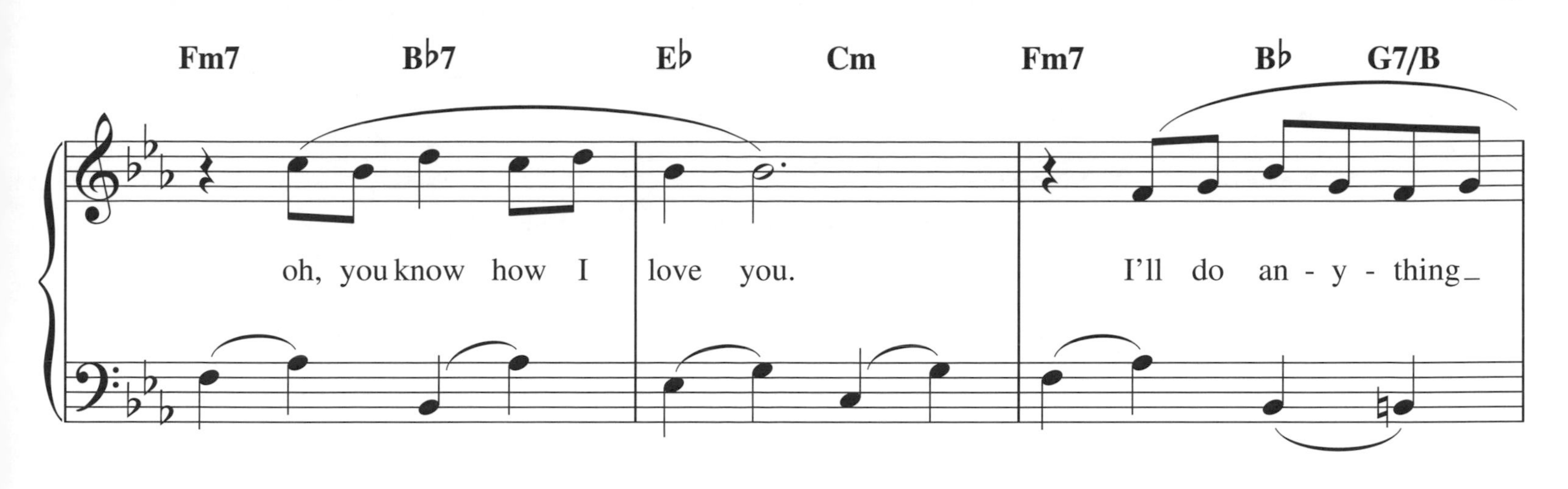
Fm7
Bb7
Eb
Cm
Fm7
Bb
G7/B
oh, you know how I love you.
I'll do an - y - thing

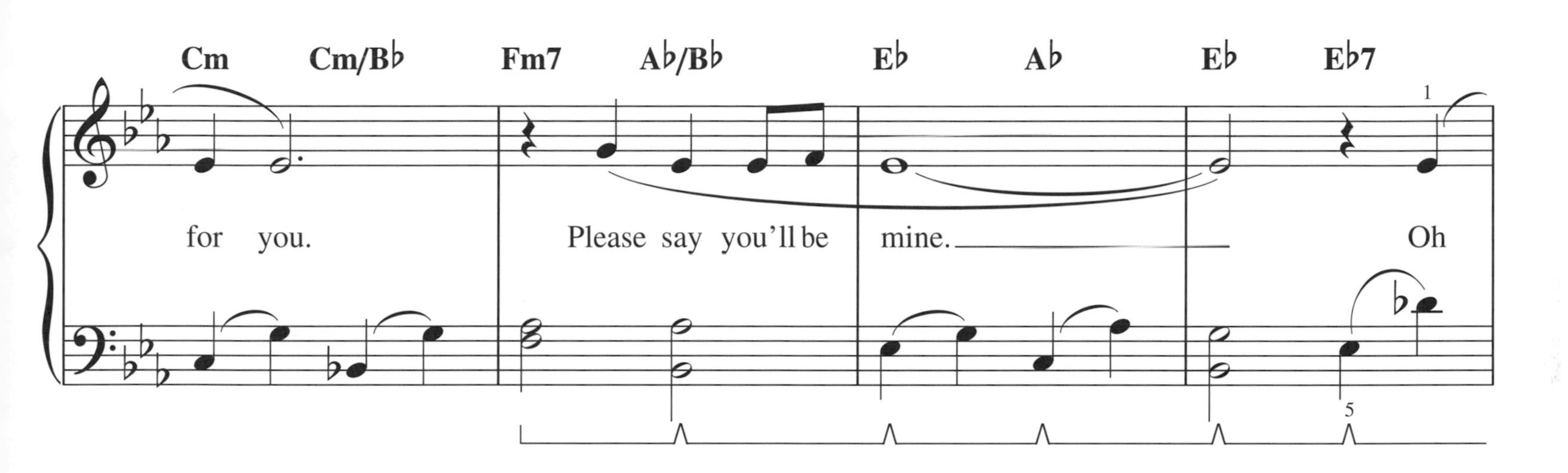
Cm
Cm/Bb
Fm7
Ab/Bb
Eb
Ab
Eb
Eb7
for you.
Please say you'll be mine.
Oh

Ab
Abm
Eb
Lord, won't you tell me why I love that girl - ic

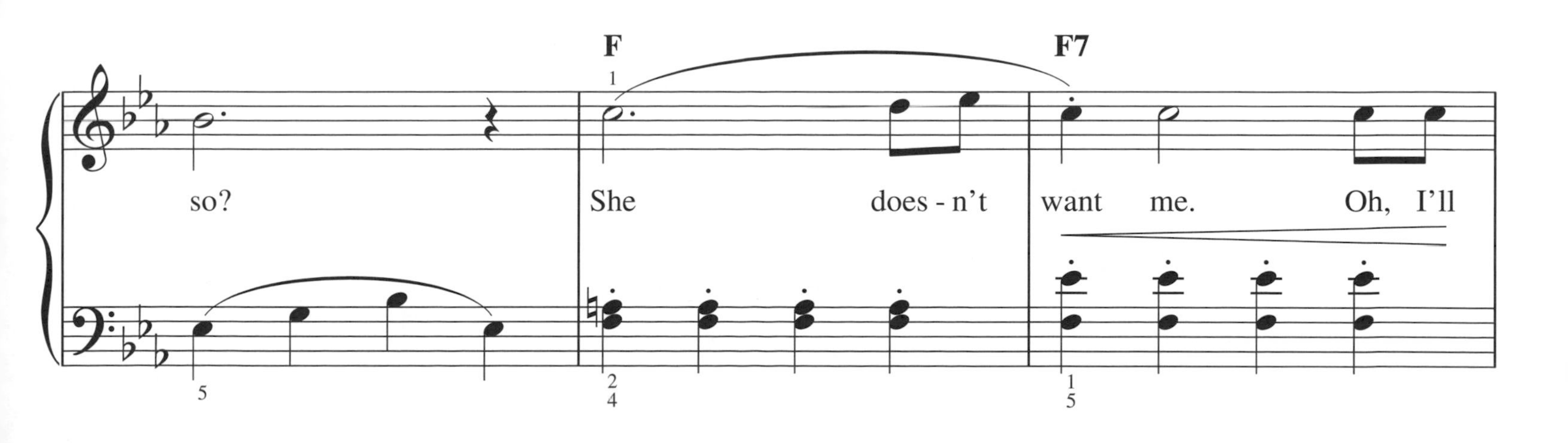
F
F7
so?
She does - n't want me.
Oh, I'll

Bb7
Eb
Cm
nev - er, nev - er, nev - er, nev - er
let you go.
Sin - cere - ly,
f
Fm7
Bb7
Eb
Cm
Fm7
Bb
G7/B
mf
oh, you know how I
love you.
I'll do an - y - thing
Cm
Cm/Bb
Fm7
Ab/Bb
Eb
Cm
Fm7
Ab/Bb
for you.
Please say you'll be
mine.
Oh, say you'll be
Eb
Cm
Fm7
Bb7
Eb6
mine.

SMOKE GETS IN YOUR EYES

from ROBERTA

Words by OTTO HARBACH
Music by JEROME KERN
Arranged by Phillip Keveren

D
F♯m7
Fdim7
Em7
A7
D/F♯
F♯7
They said some-day you'll find all who love are blind.
mp
G
G♯dim
F♯m/A
Bm7
Em7
A7
When your heart's on fire, you must re - al - ize smoke gets in your
D
Gm7
D
B♭
eyes.
So I chaffed them, and I
mf
Gm7
Dm7
D♭7
Cm7
F7
gai - ly laughed to think they could doubt my love.

Bb
Gm7
A7
Dmaj7
D#dim7
Yet to - day, my love has flown a - way, I am with - out my
Em7
A7b9
D
F#m7
Fdim7
Em7
A7
love.
Now, laugh-ing friends de - ride tears I can - not
mp
D/F#
F#7
G
G#dim
F#m/A
Bm7
hide, so I smile and say, "When a love-ly flame
Em7
A7
D
Gm7
D
D6/9
dies, smoke gets in your eyes."
rit.
pp

TEACH ME TONIGHT

Words by SAMMY CAHN
Music by GENE DePAUL
Arranged by Phillip Keveren

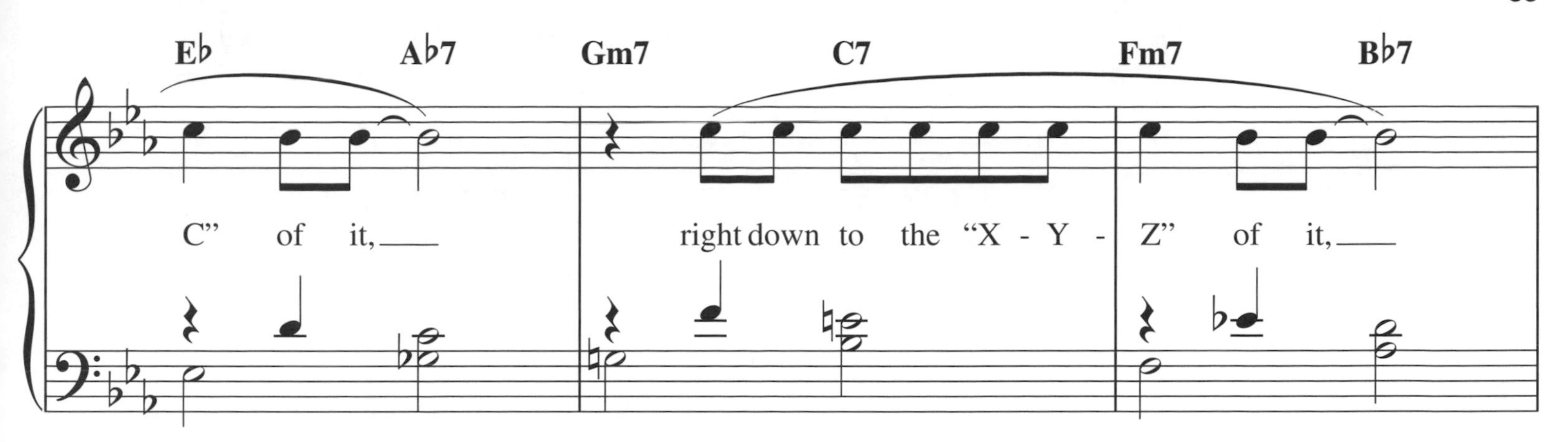
E♭ A♭7 Gm7 C7 Fm7 B♭7
C" of it, right down to the "X - Y - Z" of it,

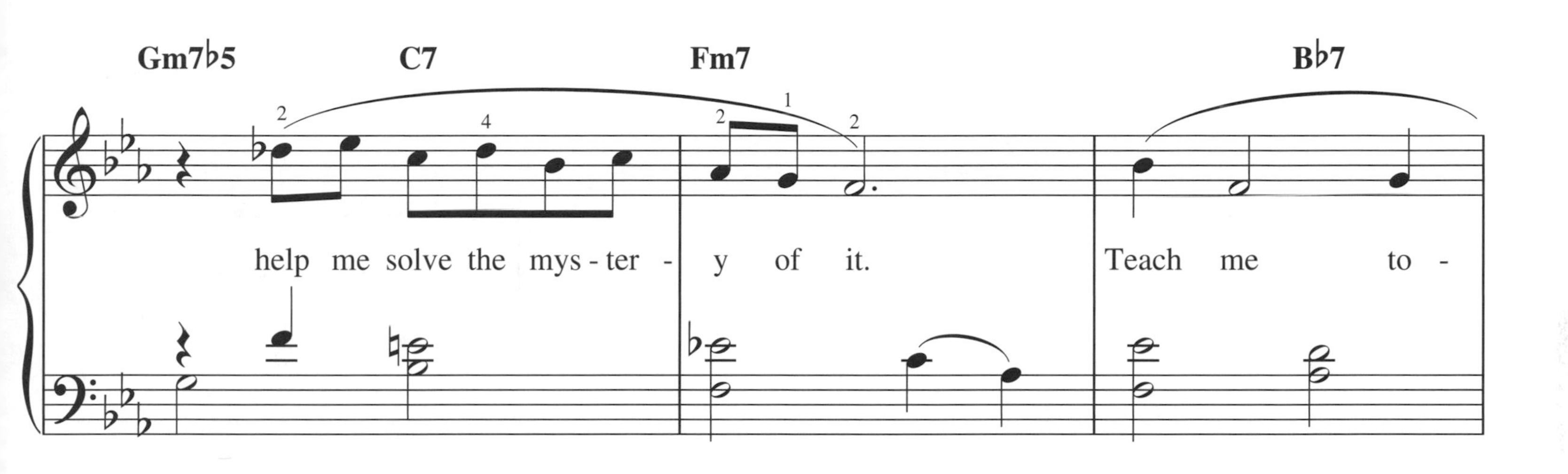
Gm7♭5 C7 Fm7 B♭7
help me solve the mys - ter - y of it. Teach me to -

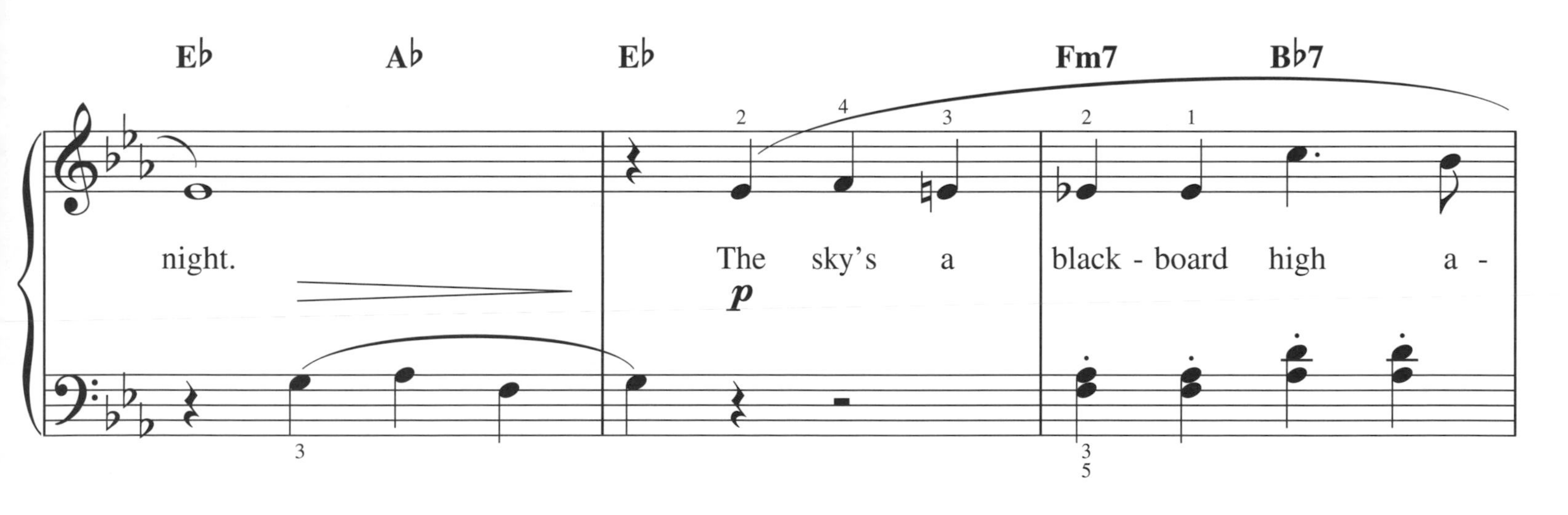
E♭ A♭ E♭ Fm7 B♭7
night. The sky's a black - board high a -
p

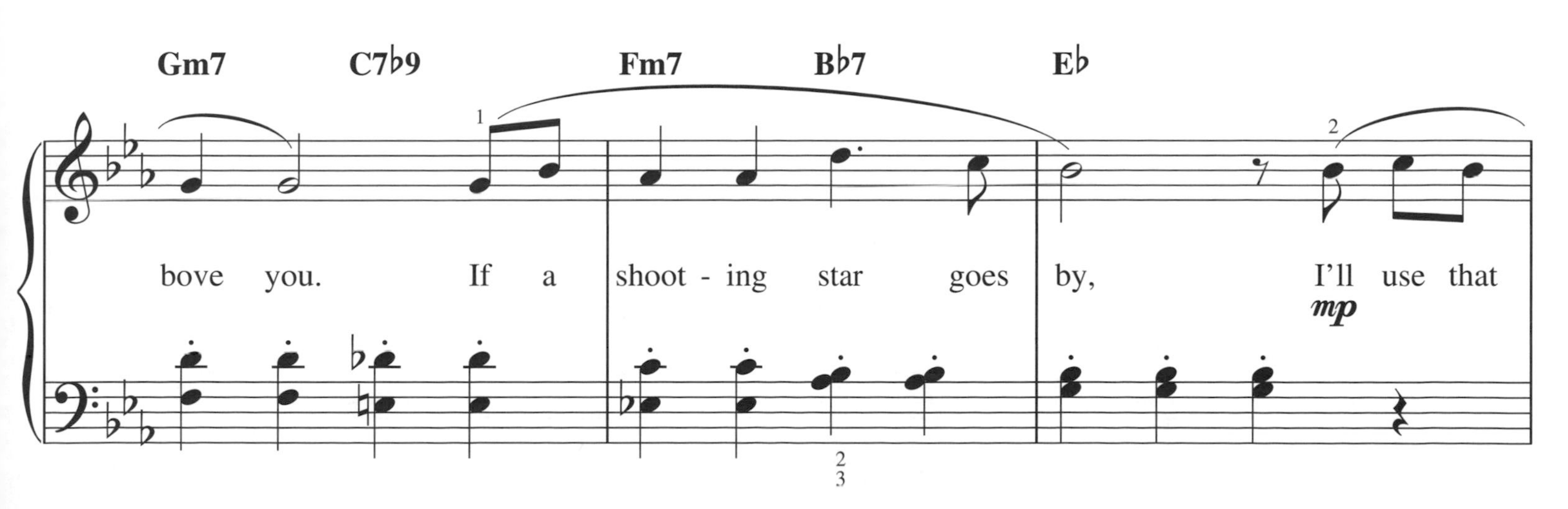
Gm7 C7♭9 Fm7 B♭7 E♭
bove you. If a shoot - ing star goes by, I'll use that
mp

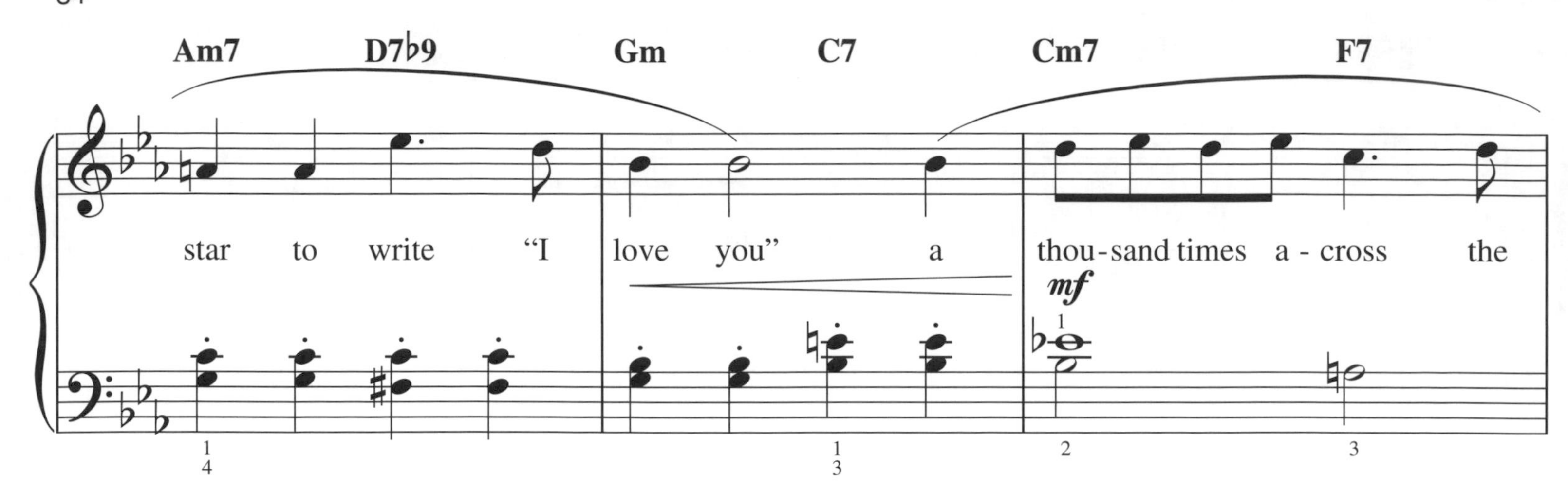
Am7
D7♭9
Gm
C7
Cm7
F7
star to write "I love you" a thou-sand times a-cross the
mf

Fm7
B♭7
E♭
A♭7
Gm7
C7
sky. One thing is-n't ver-y clear, my love, should the teach-er stand so

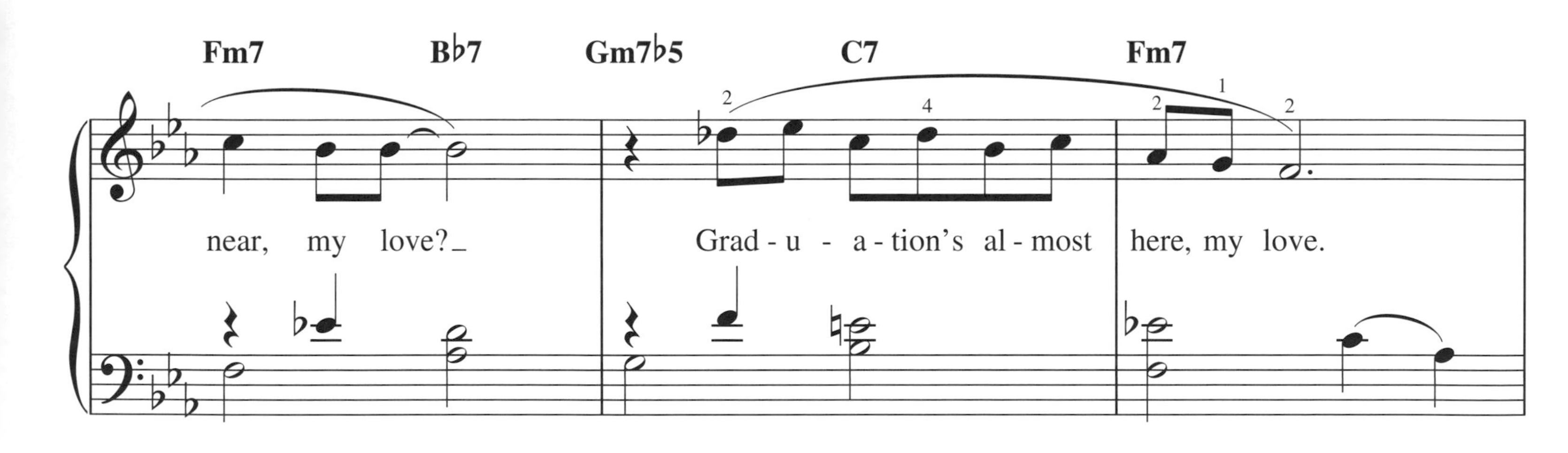
Fm7
B♭7
Gm7♭5
C7
Fm7
near, my love? Grad-u-a-tion's al-most here, my love.

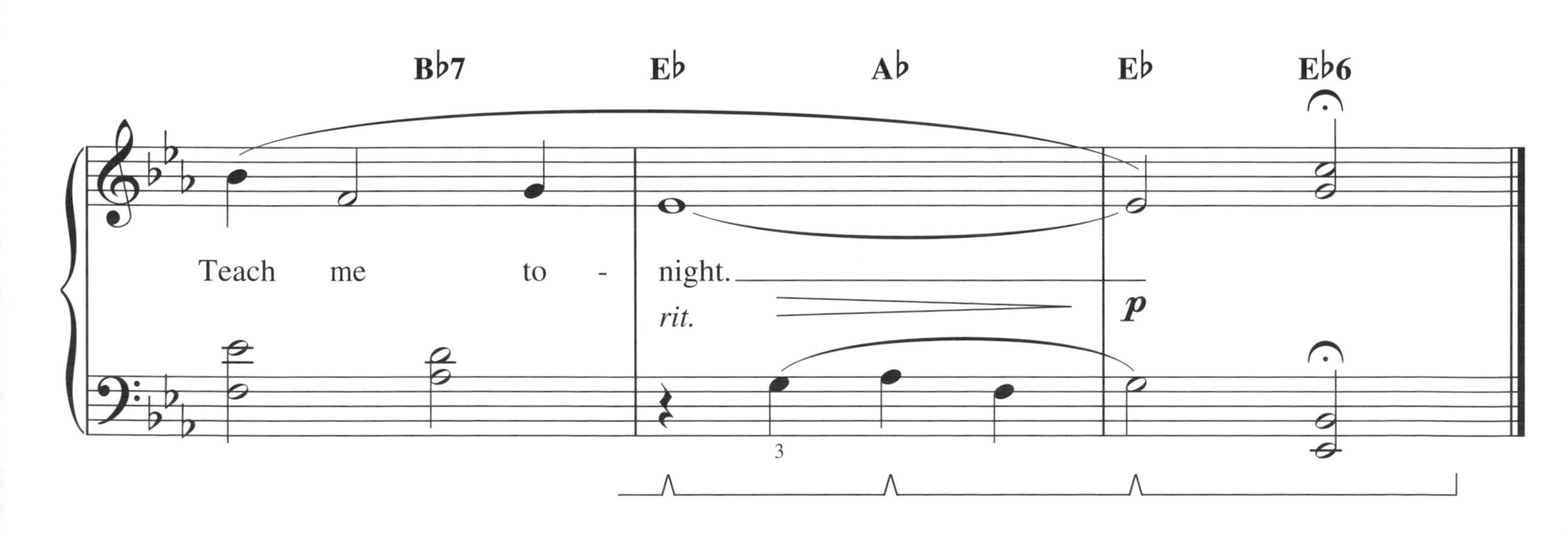
B♭7
E♭
A♭
E♭
E♭6
Teach me to-night.
rit.
p

UNCHAINED MELODY

Lyric by HY ZARET
Music by ALEX NORTH
Arranged by Phillip Keveren

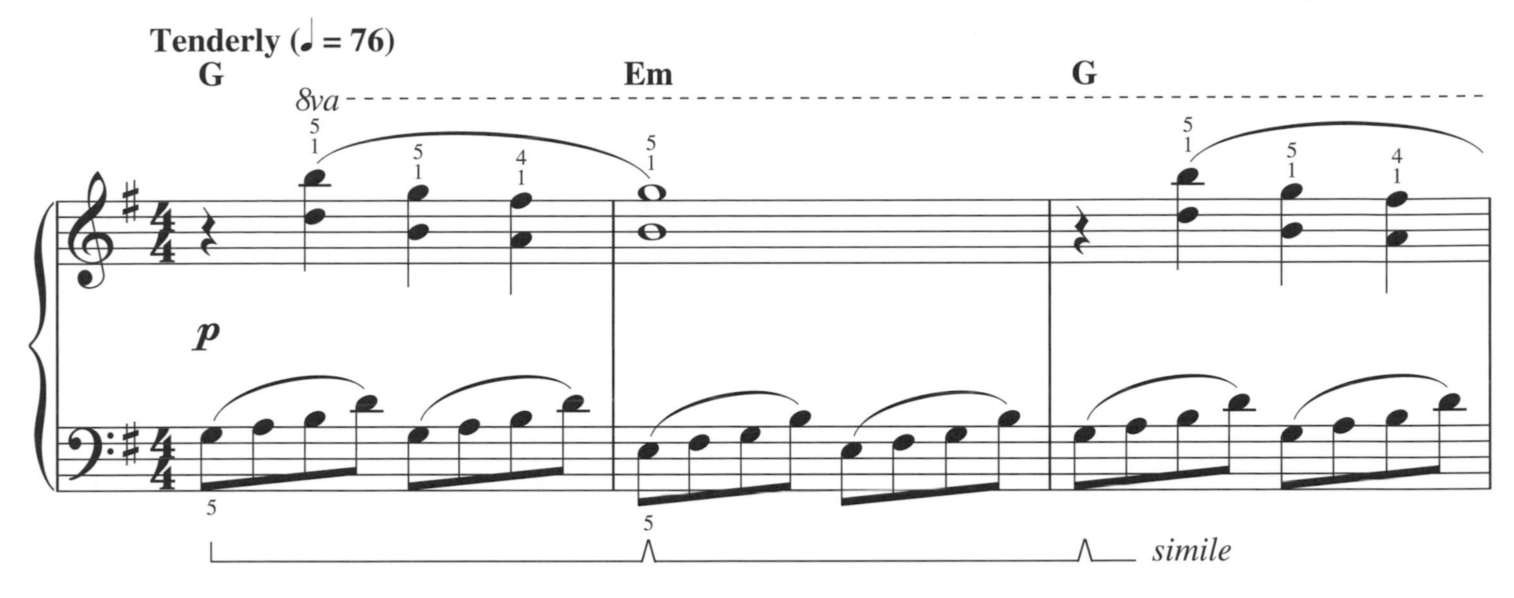

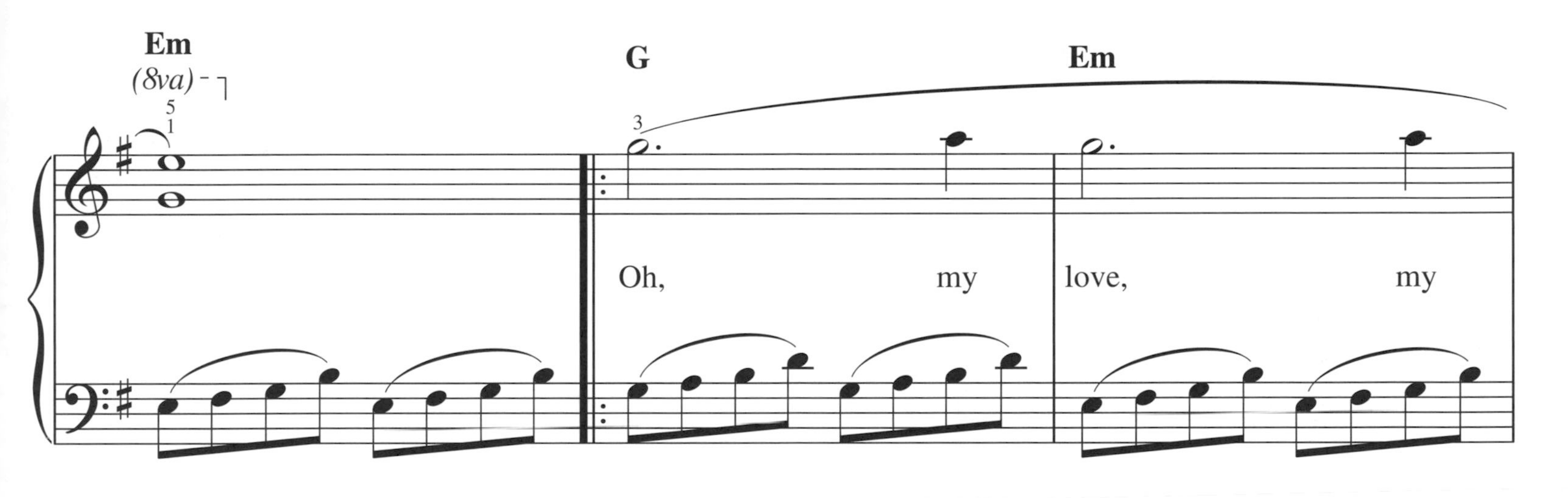

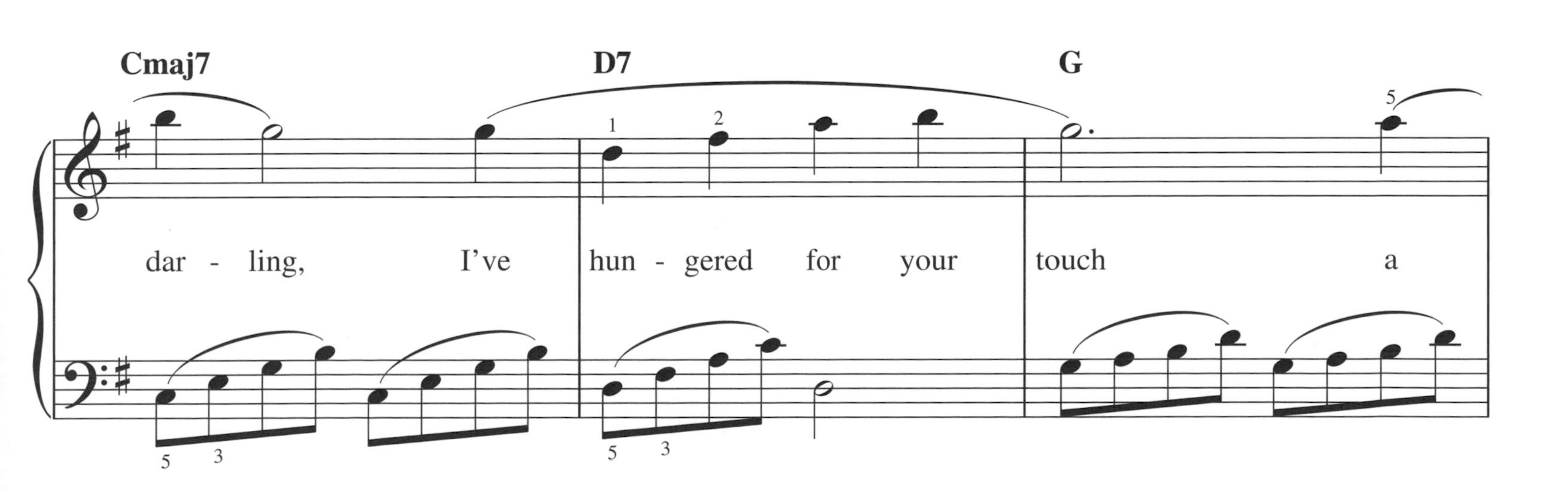

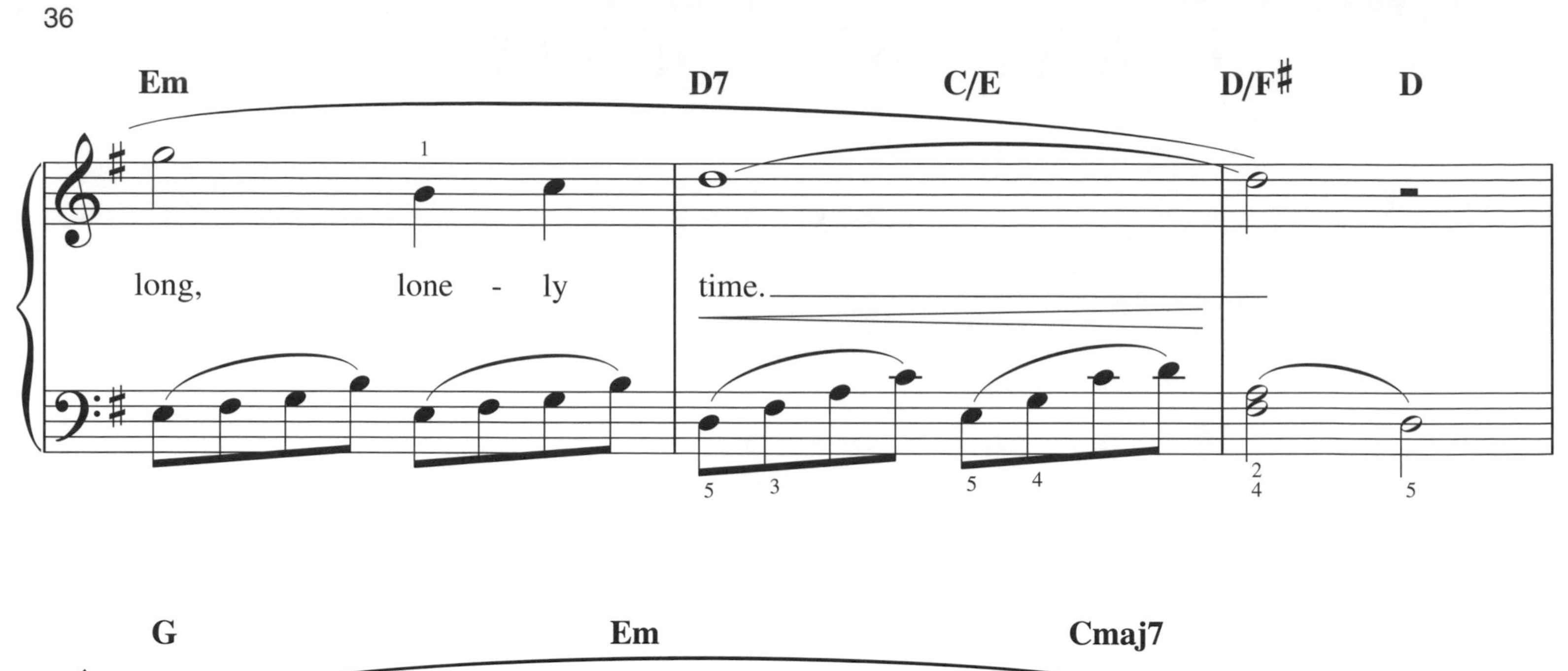
Em
D7
C/E
D/F♯
D
long, lone - ly time.

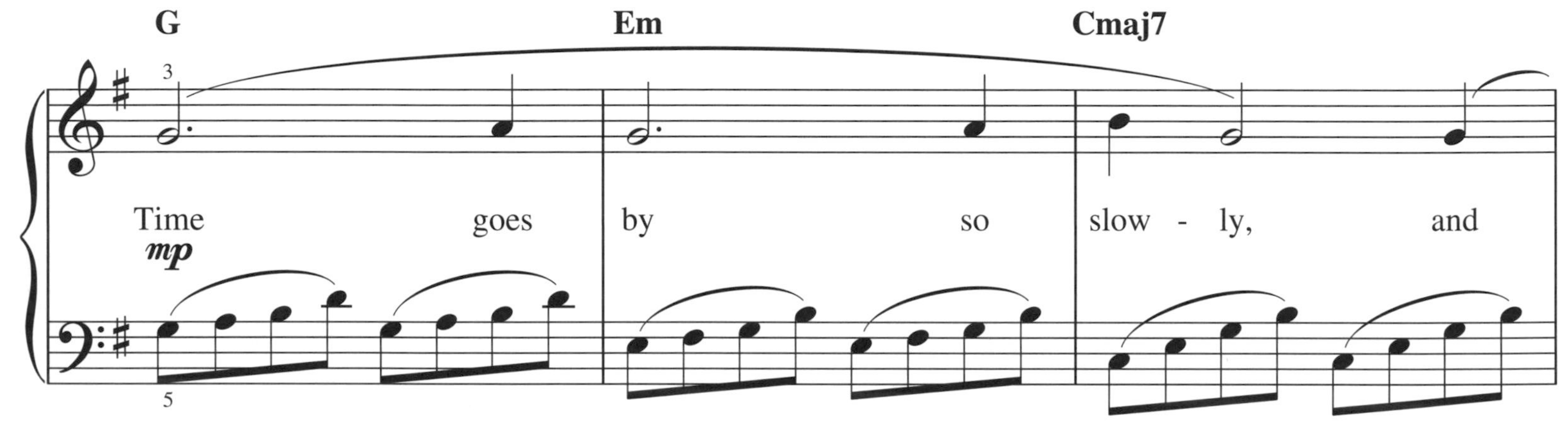
G
Em
Cmaj7
Time goes by so slow - ly, and
mp

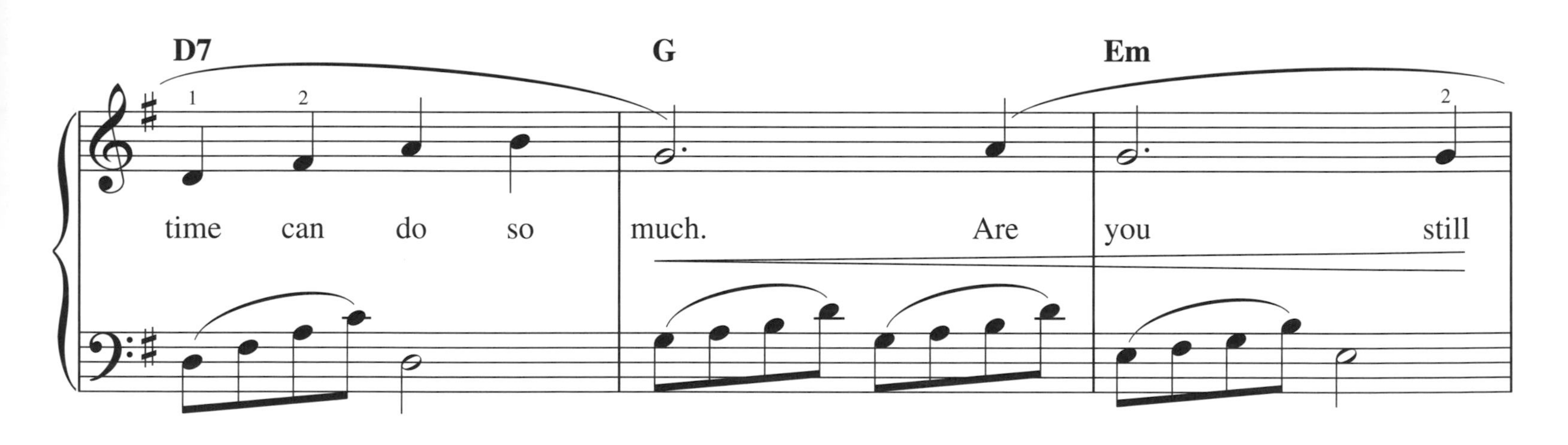
D7
G
Em
time can do so much. Are you still

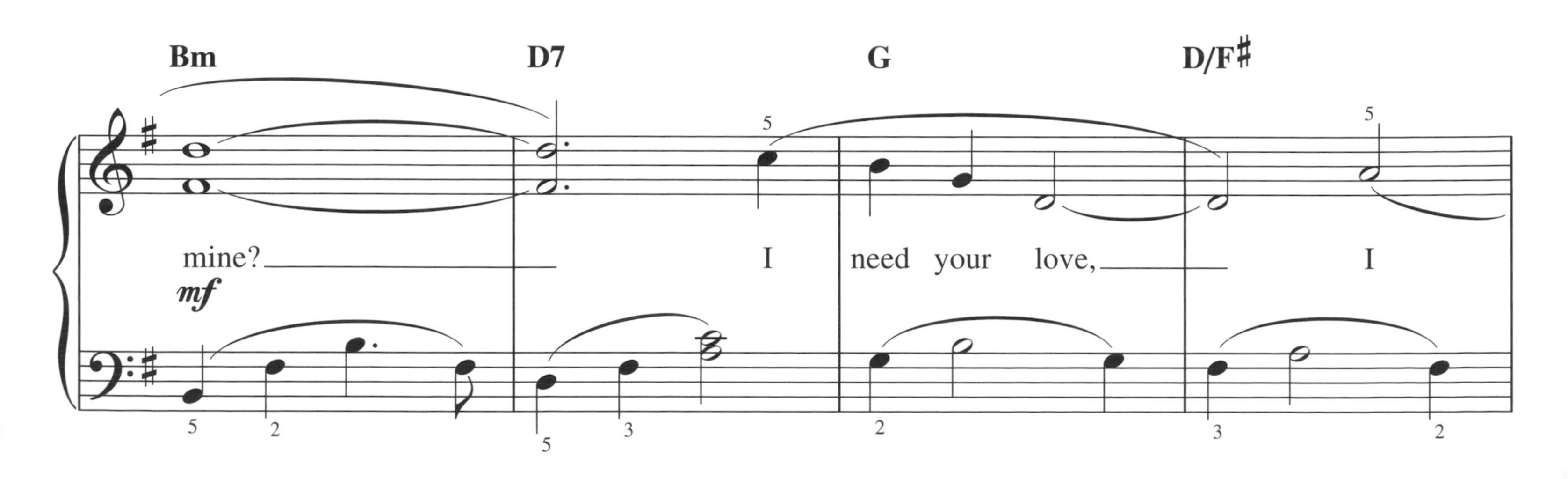
Bm
D7
G
D/F♯
mine? I need your love, I
mf

Em
Bm/D
Am/C
need your love,
God
speed your love
D7
1.
G
to
me.
p
2.
G
Em
G
8va
me.
p
Em
(8va)
G
rit.
pp

VENUS

Words and Music by
EDWARD MARSHALL
Arranged by Phillip Keveren

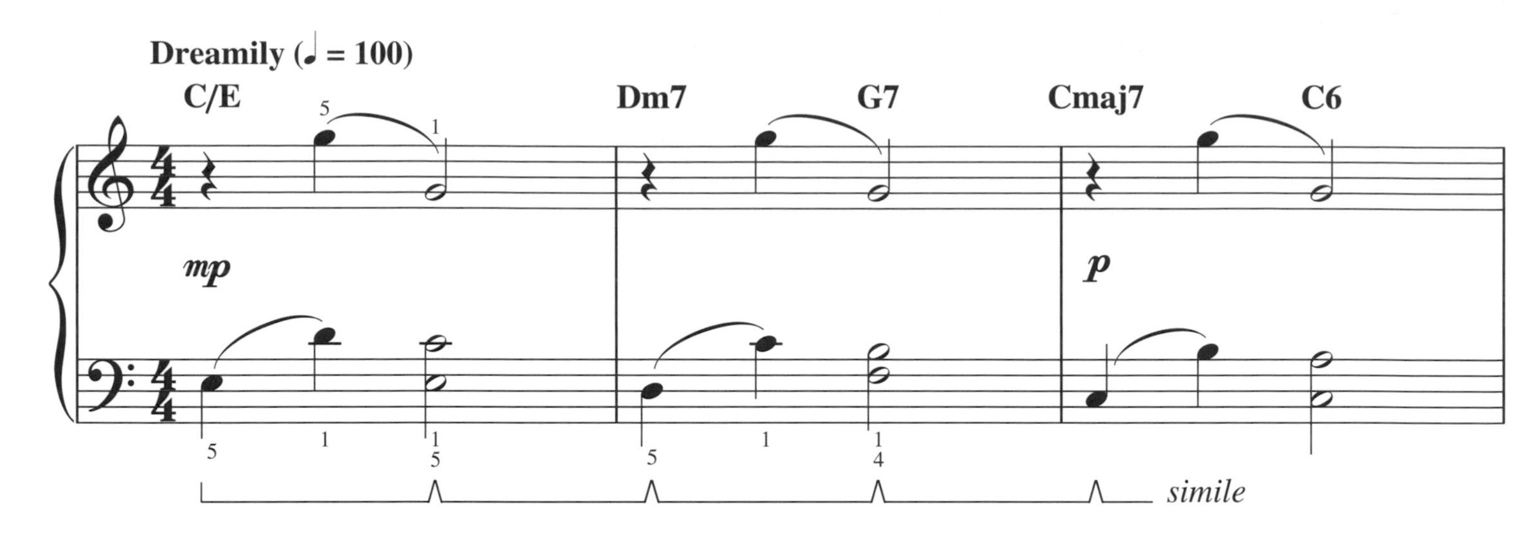

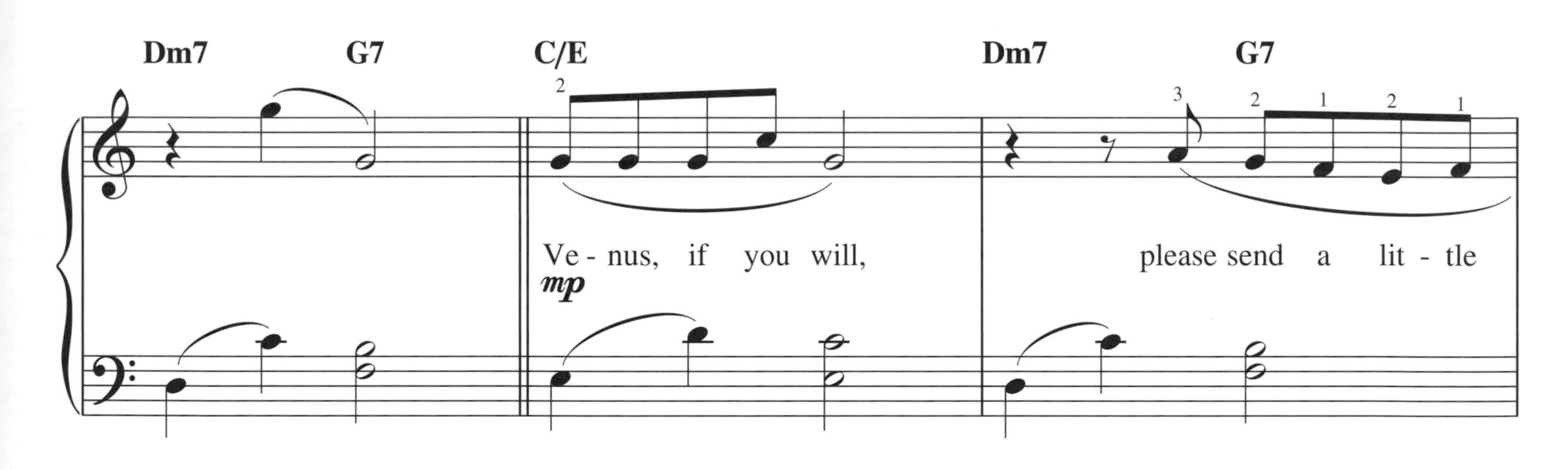

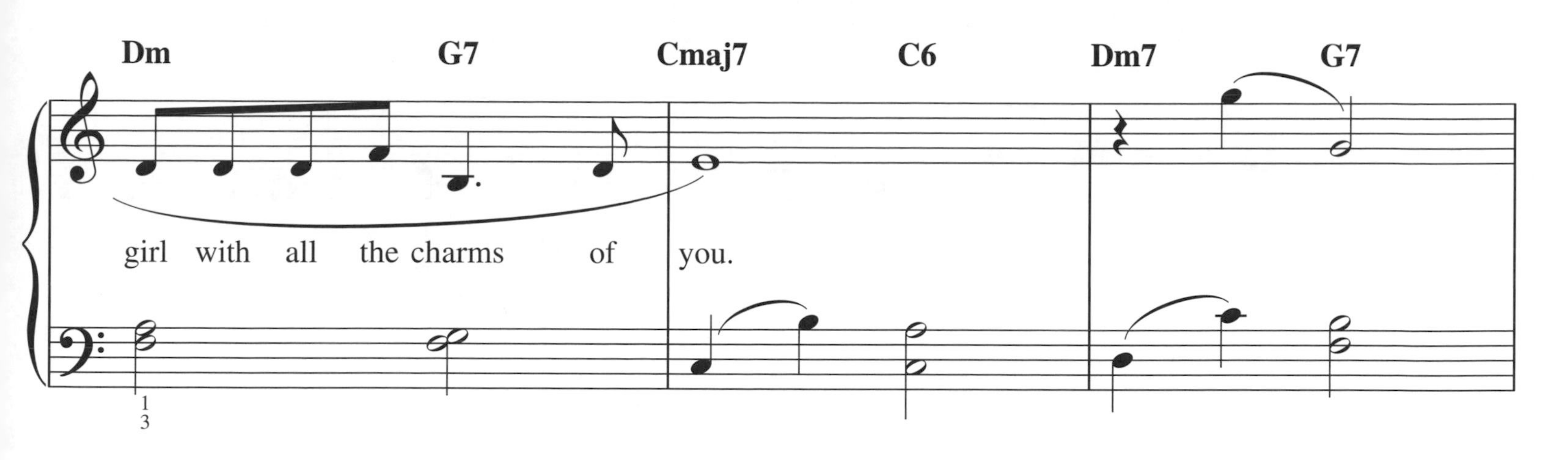
Dm
G7
Cmaj7
C6
Dm7
G7
girl with all the charms of you.

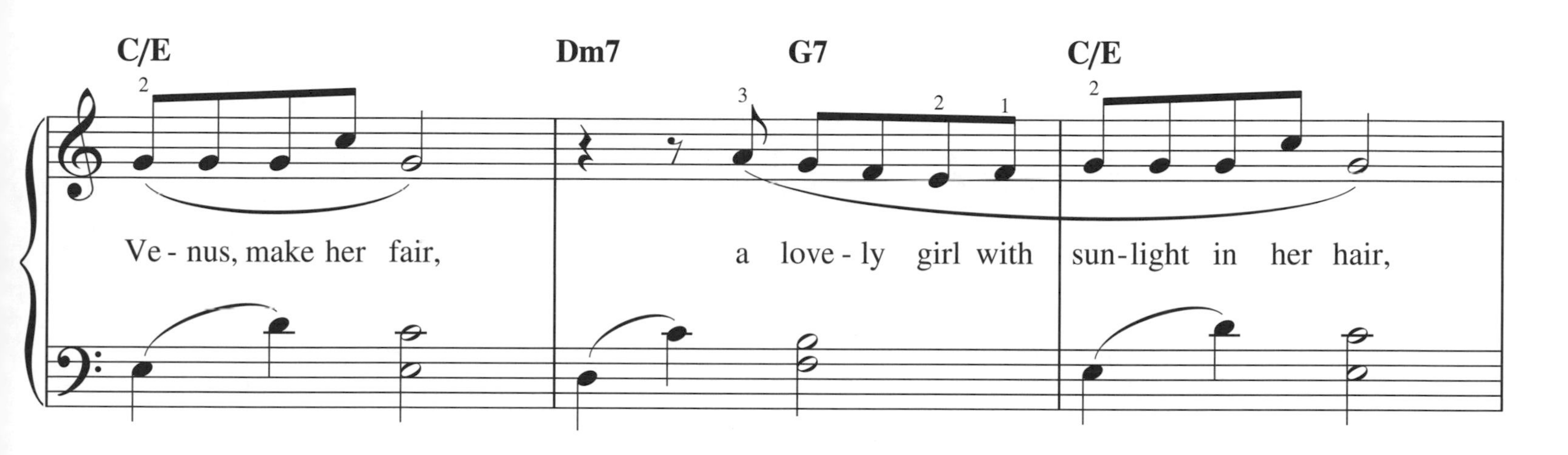
C/E
Dm7
G7
C/E
Ve - nus, make her fair, a love - ly girl with sun-light in her hair,

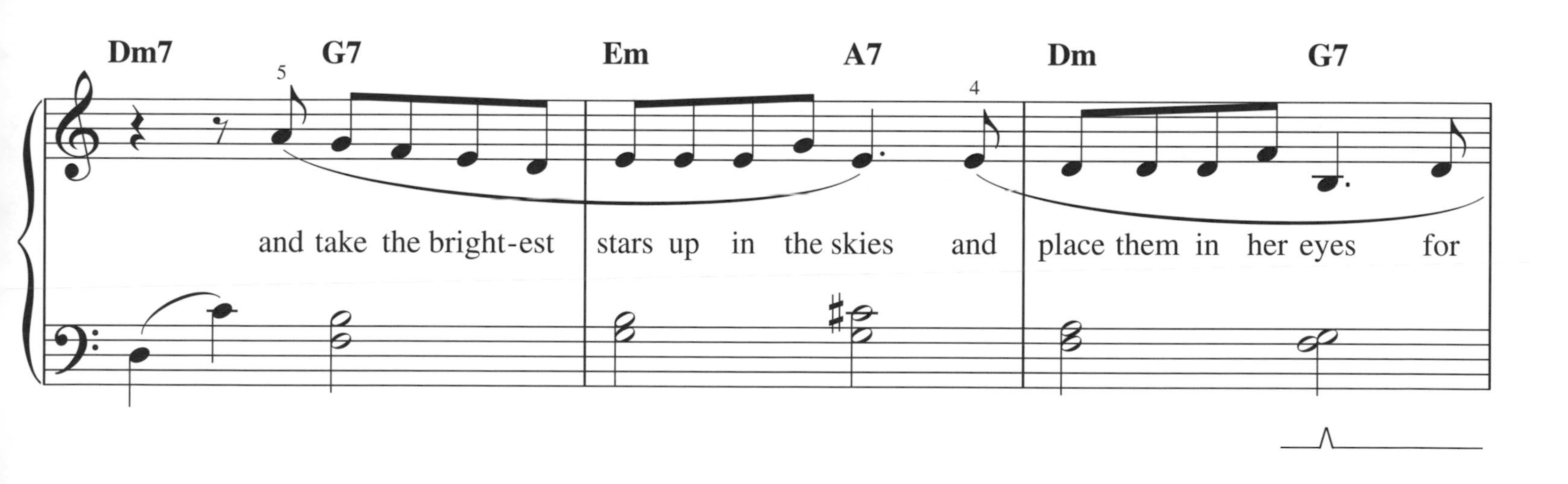
Dm7
G7
Em
A7
Dm
G7
and take the bright-est stars up in the skies and place them in her eyes for

C6
F
me.
Ve - nus,
mf

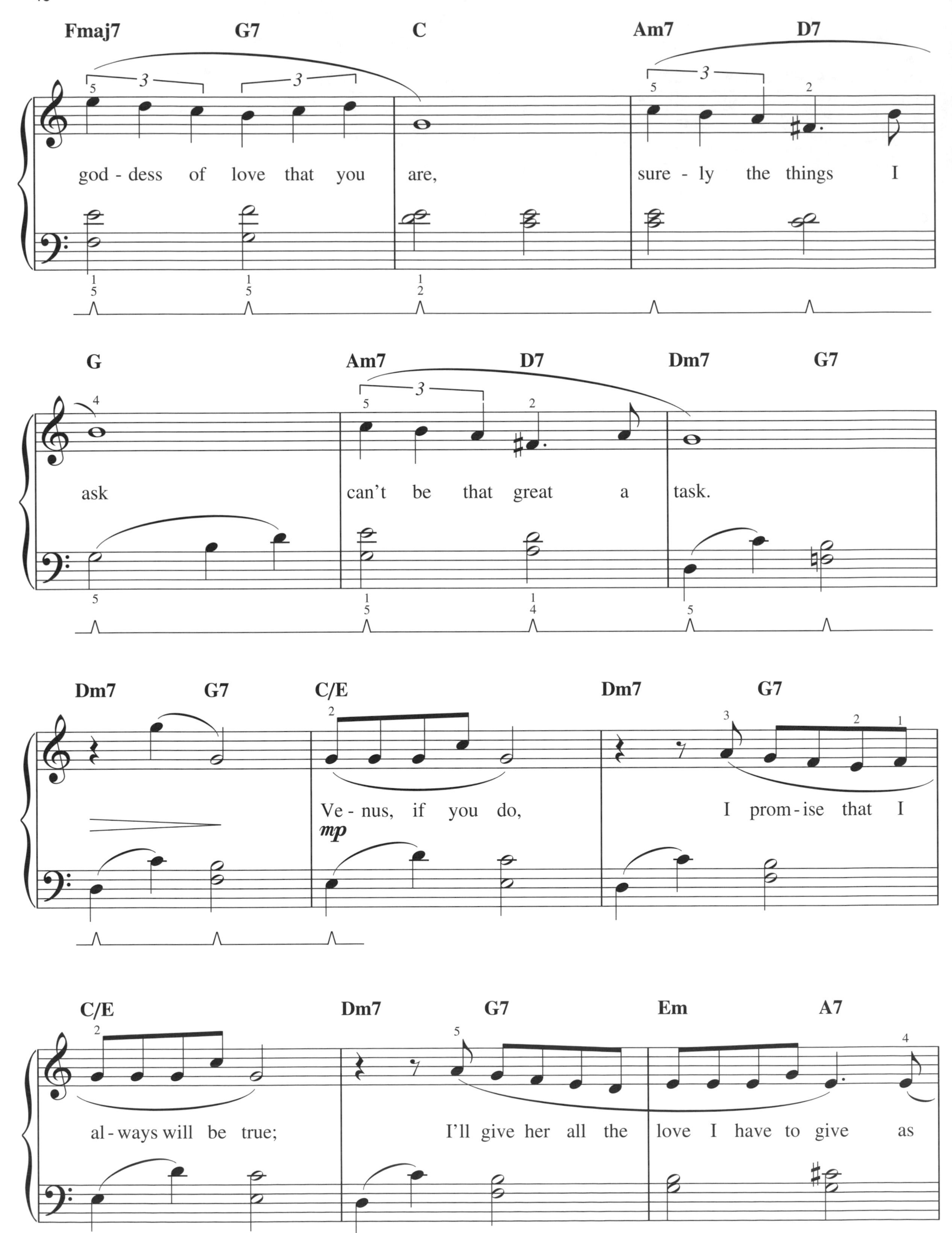
Fmaj7 G7 C Am7 D7
god - dess of love that you are, sure - ly the things I
G Am7 D7 Dm7 G7
ask can't be that great a task.
Dm7 G7 C/E Dm7 G7
Ve - nus, if you do, I prom - ise that I
mp
C/E Dm7 G7 Em A7
al - ways will be true; I'll give her all the love I have to give as

Dm
G7
C6
long as we both shall live.
Hey,
mf
Cmaj7
Fmaj7
Em7
Ve - nus,
oh,
f
Ve - nus,
Dm7
G7
C/G
Dm7
G7
make my wish come
true.
mp
C/E
Dm7
G7
Cmaj7
p
rit.

YOUNG AT HEART

Words by CAROLYN LEIGH
Music by JOHNNY RICHARDS
Arranged by Phillip Keveren

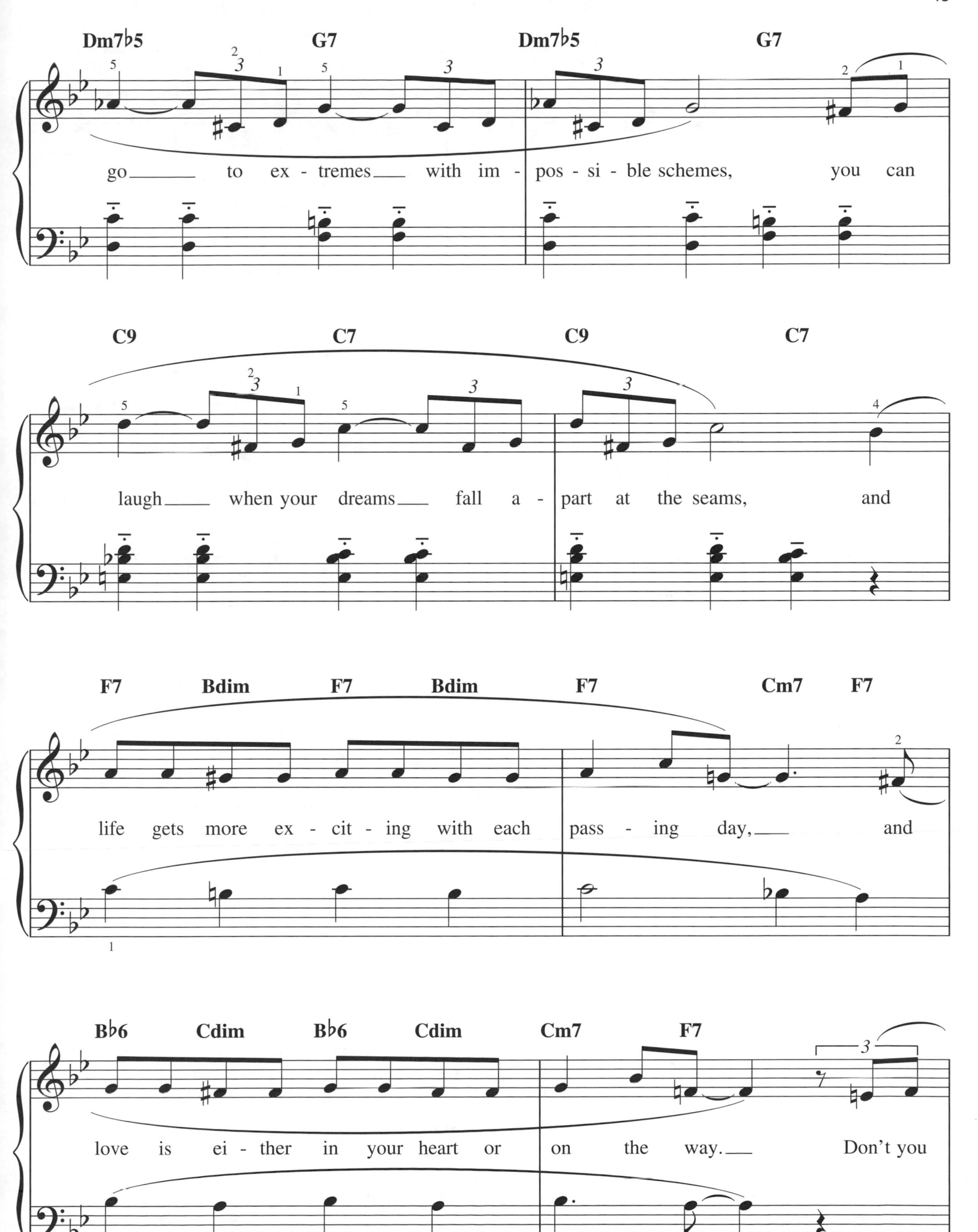
Dm7♭5 G7 Dm7♭5 G7
go to ex - tremes with im - pos - si - ble schemes, you can
C9 C7 C9 C7
laugh when your dreams fall a - part at the seams, and
F7 Bdim F7 Bdim F7 Cm7 F7
life gets more ex - cit - ing with each pass - ing day, and
B♭6 Cdim B♭6 Cdim Cm7 F7
love is ei - ther in your heart or on the way. Don't you

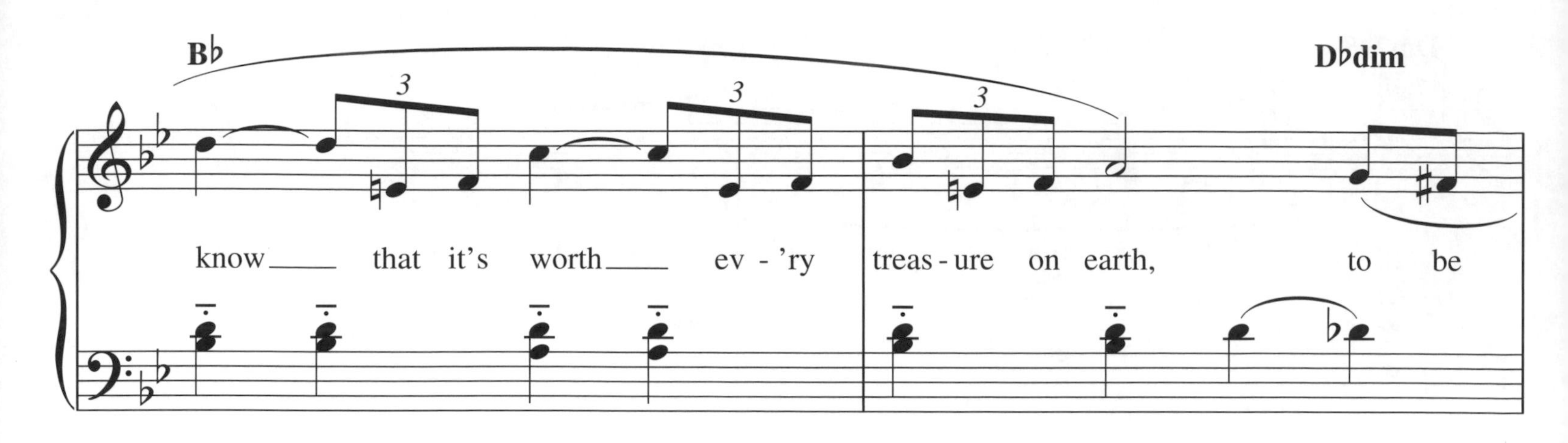
B♭
D♭dim
3
3
3
know that it's worth ev - 'ry treas - ure on earth, to be

Cm7
F
Cm7
3
3
3
young at heart? For, as rich as you are, it's much

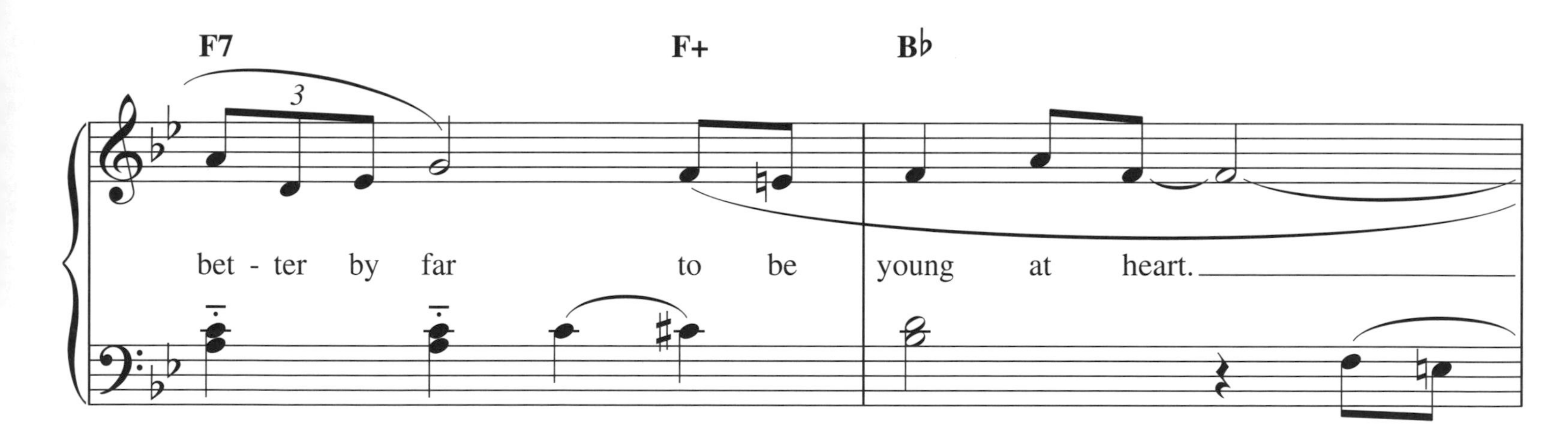
F7
F+
B♭
3
bet - ter by far to be young at heart.

Dm7♭5
G7
3
3
3
And if you should sur - vive to a

Dm7♭5
G7
C9
C7
hun-dred and five, look at all you'll de-rive out of
E♭
E♭m
B♭/F
be-ing a-live. And here is the best part,
F7
B♭
B♭/D
E♭
Edim
you have a head start if you are a-mong the ver-y
E♭/F
B♭
N.C.
E♭/F
B♭
young at heart.

WHAT A DIFF'RENCE A DAY MADE

English Words by STANLEY ADAMS
Music and Spanish Words by MARIA GREVER
Arranged by Phillip Keveren

A7
Dm(sus2)
Dm
to - day I'm part of you, dear, my lone - ly nights are

Dm7
G7
Dm7
G7
through, dear, since you said you were mine.
mf

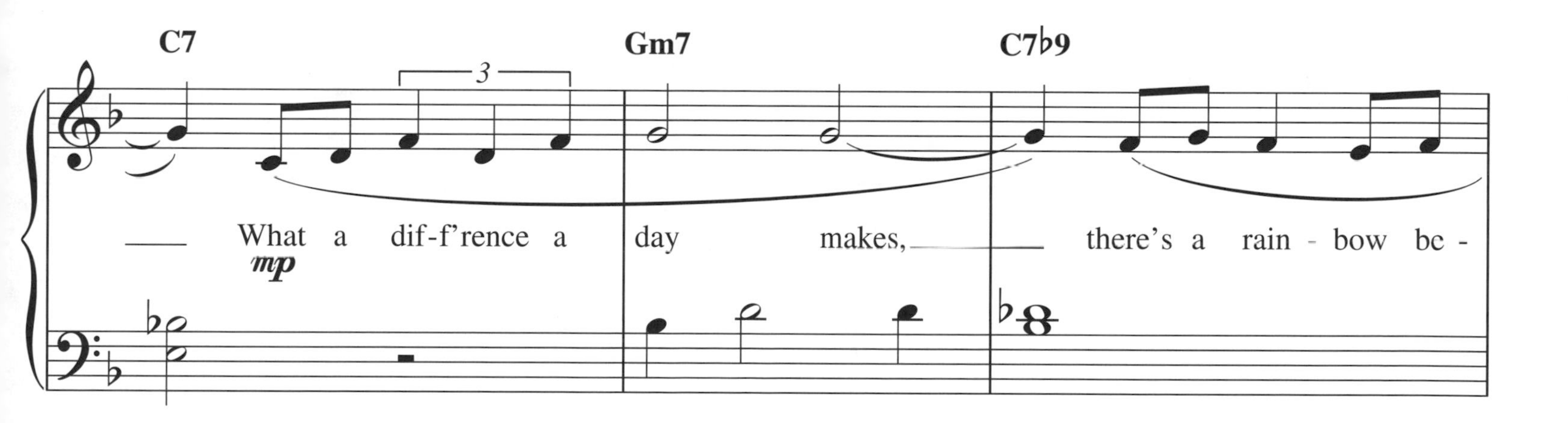
C7
Gm7
C7♭9
What a dif-f'rence a day makes, there's a rain - bow be -
mp

Fmaj7
F6
Gm7
fore me, skies a - bove can't be storm - y

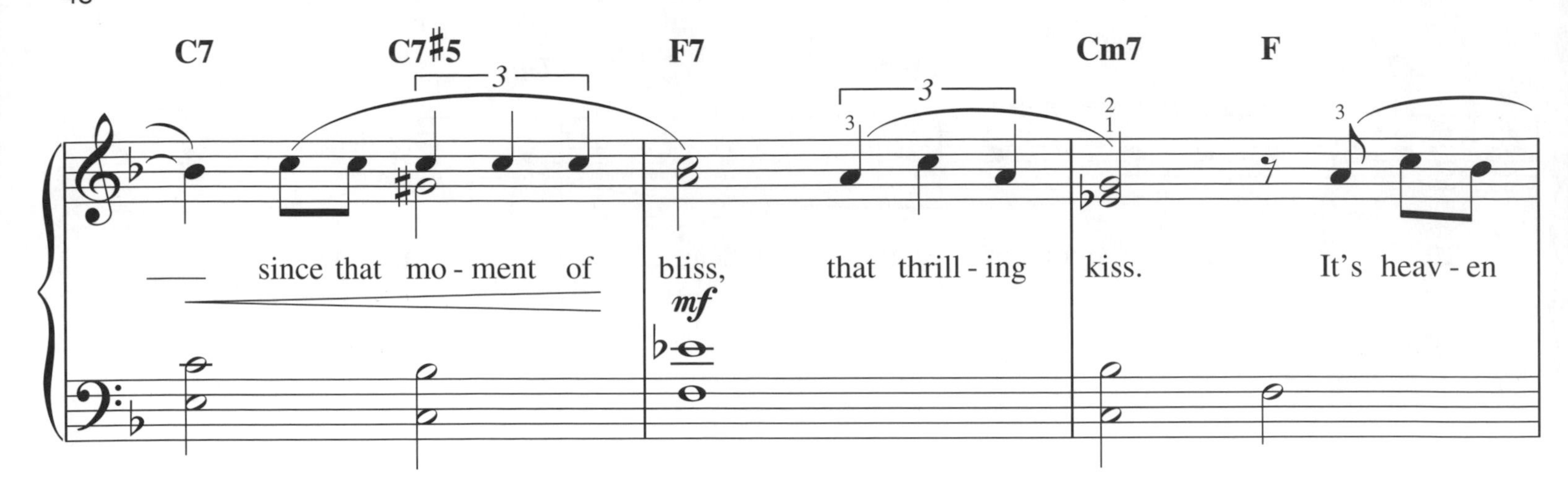
C7
C7♯5
F7
Cm7
F
since that mo - ment of
bliss,
that thrill - ing
kiss.
It's heav - en
mf

B♭maj7
B♭m(maj7)
Am7
when
you
find
ro - mance on your
men
-
u.

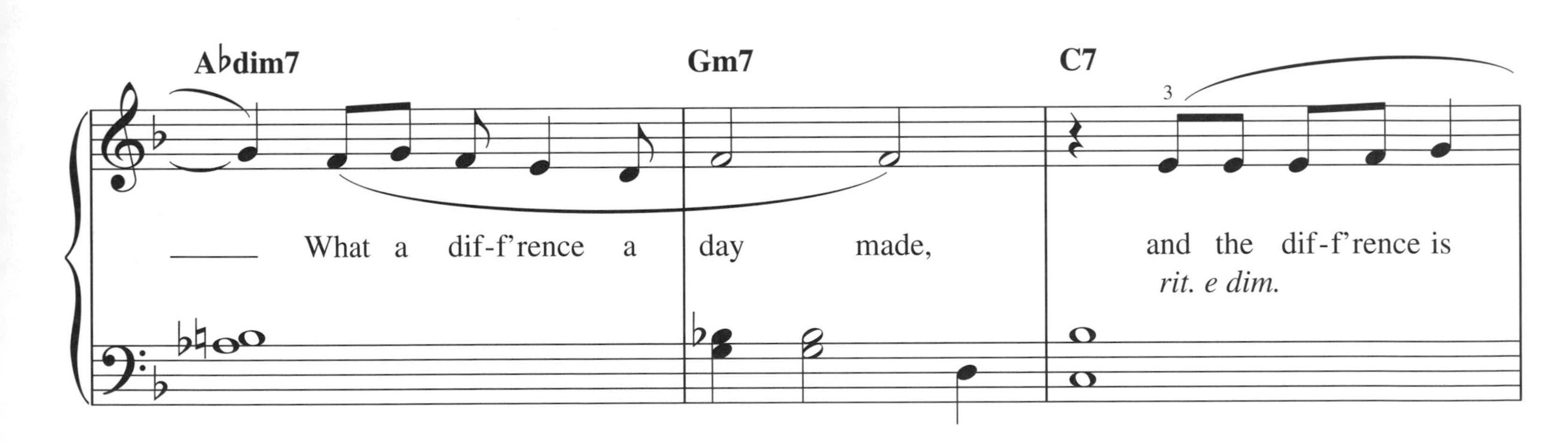
A♭dim7
Gm7
C7
What a dif-f'rence a
day
made,
and the dif-f'rence is
rit. e dim.

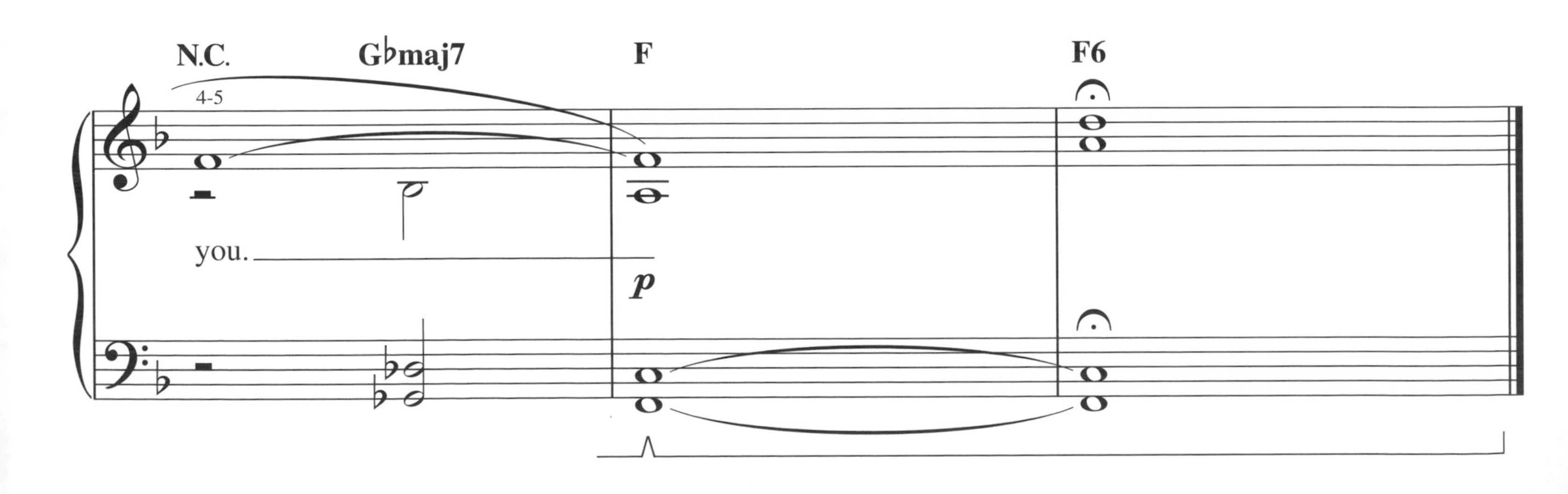
N.C.
G♭maj7
F
F6
you.
p